KU-348-499

OLD DERBY PORCELAIN

UNIFORM WITH THIS VOLUME.

OLD SPODE: A Guide for Collectors.

By Thomans G. Canon. With 57 Plates in Colour and Half-tone. Foolscap Quarto. Printed on fine Antique laid paper.

ANTIQUES AND CURIOS IN OUR HOMES.

By G. M. Vallois. New Edition with a three-coloured Frontispiece and 61 half-tone Illustrations. Foolscap 4to. (Uniform with Lewis's "Old Glass" and Gade's "Collecting Antiques for Pleasure and Profit.")

COLLECTING ANTIQUES FOR PLEASURE AND PROFIT.

By Felix Gade. 86 Illustrations printed on fine Antique paper. Foolscap 4to.

OLD GLASS, AND HOW TO COLLECT IT.

By James Sydney Lewis. 60 Illustrations in colour and half-tone, printed on fine Antique paper. Foolscap 4to.

OLD ENGLISH TOWNS.

By E. M. Lang and William Andrews. A New Edition in one volume, with a three-coloured Frontispiece and 31 Half-tone Plates. Foolscap 4to. Printed on fine Antique paper, and coloured Picture Jacket.

T. WERNER LAURIE, LTD.

D
172
F. Hurlbutt
pinx 1925.

OLD DERBY PORCELAIN

AND ITS ARTIST-WORKMEN

BY

FRANK HURLBUTT

WITH SIXTY PLATES

LONDON
T. WERNER LAURIE, LTD.
24 & 26 WATER LANE, E.C.4.
MCMXXVIII

AUTHOR'S NOTE.

The author wishes to explain that he has certain theories as to how a book of this class should be produced.

The publishers have kindly allowed him carte-blanche in this matter and the author alone is responsible for anything unconventional in the make-up of this volume.

SECOND IMPRESSION

PRINTED IN GREAT BRITAIN BY
THE DUNEDIN PRESS LIMITED, EDINBURGH

TO M.

BEST OF SISTERS

WHO CARES LITTLE FOR OLD PORCELAIN

BUT MORE FOR THE AUTHOR

THIS BOOK IS INAPPROPRIATELY

BUT AFFECTIONATELY

DEDICATED.

CONTENTS

CHAPTER PAGE

I. A Short History of Old Derby Porcelain 3

II. The Modellers and Figure-Makers of Old Derby Porcelain . . 25

III. The Flower Painters on Old Derby Porcelain 55

IV. The Figure-Subject Painters on Old Derby Porcelain 85

V. The Landscape Painters on Old Derby Porcelain 105

VI. The Bird and Fruit Painters on Old Derby Porcelain 129

VII. A Chronology of Old Derby Porcelain 145

References 161

PREFACE

Old Derby Porcelain appeals to one in a special manner; in a way in which Old Chelsea, Bow, Worcester, &c. do not; inasmuch as there is a personality, an individuality in the making and decorating of this porcelain which is lacking in others.

Its founder, William Duesbury I, owed nothing to patrons, Royal or otherwise; nothing to education or to position.

He was a workman pure and simple, the son of a working currier.

As a boy he was apprenticed to his trade of china ware painting, and worked his way up, step by step, to be a small employer, then to be a manufacturer, finally to be the owner of the largest business of its kind in the whole kingdom.

In like manner his workmen-artists have an individuality of their own, which (except in rare individual instances) is wanting in all the other porcelain factories.

Preface

One can take up a piece of Derby porcelain and can say with certainty "This is the work of Withers, of Boreman, of Billingsley, of Pegg the Quaker. This piece has been modelled by Spängler, by Stephan, moulded and tooled by Joseph Hill, by Isaac Farnsworth."

Of what other factory can one say this? except perhaps of some of the later porcelain made in the nineteenth century.

It is to enable readers to recognise the artist-workman by his work on specimens of Old Derby Porcelain, whether in their own collections, in the museums, or in the dealers' shops, the sales of old china, or wherever else the chase, the thrilling pursuit, of such specimens may take them, that this work is written.

And to a Collector how much this knowledge increases not only the interest, but also the value, of an old Derby piece.

One may have a beautiful old picture, or a fine statue, which may be something which is charming and artistically satisfying; but if one knows not the artist or the sculptor, it has lost nine-tenths of its interest and value.

The examples illustrated here are selected for

the most part with the same object; many from the Author's collection.

To Mr Bernard Rackham and the Director and Secretary of the Victoria and Albert Museum, to Mr F. Williamson of the Derby Museum, Mr G. H. Wallis of the Nottingham Museum, Mr A. H. S. Bunford, and last, but not least, to my eldest sister, who has helped me with the revision and proofs, and Mr T. Werner Laurie for helpful suggestions, and to others who have helped me with photographs of pieces and kind suggestions, I give most grateful thanks.

For historical facts and much original information I am indebted to earlier writers on Old Derby Porcelain. Chiefly to Haslem, Bemrose, Moore Binns, and Jewitt.

At the same time it will be found that this work is not a mere rechauffé of old information; but that it opens up new and entrancing avenues of knowledge,[1] brings coherency into an unattached medley of isolated facts, corrects some hoary and respectable errors and, it is hoped, may set others on the road to new discoveries.

Old Derby Porcelain has been too long neglected.

Preface

The Author will welcome correspondence on any points mentioned in this work, whether to confirm or refute; above all to extend by means of new facts the general knowledge on the subject of Old Derby Porcelain.

PENYFFORDD HOUSE,
Near Chester.

CHAPTER I

A Short History of Old Derby Porcelain

CHAPTER I

A Short History of Old Derby Porcelain

All previous writers on this subject have differed very strongly both as to when porcelain, as distinguished from earthenware, was first made in Derby, and even more, if that were possible, as to who first made it.

Each has produced first-class evidence to support his own theory and to demolish those of others; but so far as the present writer can gather from their books, none has tried to advance a theory which will arrange the various pieces of evidence into a coherent whole, in which each piece of testimony, each document taken in its proper sequence, serves only to strengthen the chain of evidence and nowhere to prove the contrary.[2]

This the present writer claims to do in the following short narrative.

Within the limits of a book of this size it is impossible to marshal the evidence; nevertheless, if put to the test, it will be found that no evidence yet produced will refute, while all can be made to support, this theory.

Porcelain was first made in Derby, as in so many of the other early English factories, by a man of French extraction.

André Planché was the son of French emigrés from the North-Western districts of France; portions of which were then under the rule and dominion of Austria.

His father was a potter who had worked at Meissen and had come over from there to work in one of the Staffordshire pot works.

André (or Andrew, as it was soon anglicized), learnt from his father the art of modelling, and also how to mix the necessary earths and frits for making soft porcelain similar to those made in Lille and St. Cloud, Chantilly and Mennecy.

Andrew Planché was young and ambitious.

Tales came to the Potteries of the starting of new factories to make the beautiful translucent porcelain at Bow and at Chelsea: why not at Derby too? In 1745 Andrew Planché was seventeen years of age.[3] He modelled with spirit and life small figures of dogs and birds, of cats and cows, of sheep and goats in his porcelain clay and got them fired in a pipemaker's oven; the only one at that place which would preserve the beautiful creamy whiteness of the paste and glaze.

Shortly afterwards, probably owing to the owner of the pipekiln objecting to the trouble, and possibly loss, of firing porcelain articles belonging to another in his oven; for the temperature required to fire porcelain and pipes is not the same, the young Planché built himself a small oven in a large chimney, and obtained even better results.

These charming little pieces of porcelain attracted attention in Derby—a new thing indeed in the small Midland town—and among others they came to the notice of Mr Thos. Rivett, M.P. for the town and on two occasions its Mayor, one of the proprietors of a very rising and enterprising pottery, the Cockpit Hill Pot Works, carried on by Messrs Wm. Butts, Thos. Rivett, and John Heath.

Of these the first was a practical potter, the last a banker.

They quickly saw the possibilities of the new

porcelain. Planché was engaged, and for about eight years, from 1747 to 1755, the Cockpit Hill Pot Works turned out porcelain figures and other articles, steadily increasing in quality, quantity and importance.

How then does William Duesbury arrive on the scene?

At this time Wm. Duesbury I was carrying on a highly successful decorating works in London. China dealers in London would buy boxes full of China ware in the white from the various factories, Bow, Chelsea, Derby, &c. and have them decorated at Duesbury's in styles to suit their own ideas or the taste of their customers.

My Lord would make the Grand Tour and passing through France and Germany, would buy specimens of the porcelains of St. Cloud and of Meissen. On his return home he would order porcelain to match, or replacements, from his London china shop. My Lady would be given a charming plate or teapot from the Orient, and nothing would serve but that she must have a complete service to the same pattern. Duesbury was kept busy.

But porcelain makers got tired of seeing the

most profitable and least risky part of their trade getting into the hands of outside decorators. Capable artists, at first scarce, were becoming more numerous. Had not the London factories even roped in children from the poorhouses themselves and had them taught the art of painting.

They refused therefore to sell any more porcelain in the white. So Duesbury must seek a source of supply for himself.

His first attempt was with Wm. Littler of Longton Hall; but the latter's artistic but impracticable methods were bound to end in failure. He next approaches the Cockpit Hill Pot Works, and at a good moment. The competition of Chelsea, Bow, Worcester, Longton Hall is being felt; pottery is profitable, porcelain is not. Planché is leading a dissolute life; but can still be useful to Duesbury, who must have porcelain if he is not to lose his growing and profitable business. Heath the banker is willing to finance a man of his steady, pushing character, on terms. Premises consisting of a substantial dwelling-house for Duesbury, a row of cottages and tenements with their gardens, on the Nottingham Road, capable of being adapted for a small factory, are acquired, and in 1756 the Old Derby Factory is started.

As always, Planché, the unsteady, unreliable man of inventive genius, drops out, having put others in the way of taking his place, and Duesbury the worker, the steady, the reliable man of business, succeeds. The agreement drawn up between Heath the Capitalist, Planché the arcanist, and Duesbury the hardworking, able, honest business man, was never signed. A fresh scandal occupied Planché and disgusted Duesbury. Heath beginning to feel the monetary tightness that eventually resulted in his bankruptcy, drew in his horns, if he did not withdraw all his capital from the new venture, and Duesbury squaring his broad shoulders, gazing straight before him with those steadfast far-seeing eyes, takes on the whole new venture alone, and carries it to a triumphant conclusion.[4]

From that moment the Derby Factory on the Nottingham Road, close to St. Mary's Bridge, never looked back. Longton Hall might fail, but its failure only hastened Duesbury's success by giving him more and better trained men, models, materials.

Chelsea, Bow, even his old rival Giles's Decorating Shop at Kentish Town might dwindle and close; but he was able to absorb everything that was best in them all, and rose on their ruins to higher and greater success.

In this way, with honesty and enterprise as a business man, fair dealing and kindness as an employer, affectionate and loved in his family life, Duesbury brought his Porcelain Factory to the highest point of artistic and commercial success, and died in October, 1786, at the age of sixty-one years, leaving the finest porcelain business in the country to his son, Wm. Duesbury II.

The second Wm. Duesbury was a worthy son to such a father.—If he had not the stamina, the immense industry, the enterprise of his father, he was nevertheless well fitted to consolidate the position gained and to maintain it in all respects. Unfortunately he was not a man of robust health. —It was only a year before his father died that, feeling his health failing, he took his son William II into partnership; and barely ten years later in 1796 Wm. Duesbury II died, having taken into partnership an Irishman of the name of Michael

Kean, who had been recommended to him by his London Agent as a man of artistic taste and business enterprise and who had been coming to the fore in London as a miniature painter. This was in 1795.

After Wm. Duesbury II's death Michael Kean carried on the business for the widow, the young heir Wm. Duesbury III, and the family.

Apparently he did it well, and incidentally he married the widow.

Wm. Duesbury III was a boy of nine when his father died. At first therefore all the management of the business was in Kean's hands.

From an artistic point of view he maintained its character for excellence. It was during his management that the wonderful waxen biscuit body, so much valued by collectors, was invented, though Collectors not knowing anything about manufacture, think that the gloss that is found upon the finest specimens was an attribute of the paste, whereas it was not, but was formed by firing the figure or group in a freshly glazed saggar—the volatilized elements of the glaze during the firing being then partially absorbed by the soft body, with the charming and artistic result now so much appreciated.

Contrary too to the opinion advanced by some writers, it was Kean, not Bloor, who first introduced the popular if inartistic Japan patterns, viz. :—Old Japan, Rock Japan, Witches Japan, Exeter Japan, Grecian Japan, and Rose Japan, which survive to this day.

One result of Duesbury II's illness and death and Kean's taking up the reins of authority was that a number of Duesbury Ist's old hands left. They could not stand the new master and his new methods.

Billingsley the best flower painter, Boreman the best landscape painter, Jockey Hill another fine landscape painter, Banford the best figure subject painter, and others, all left about this time, and Kean had to replace them by hook or by crook—and very well he did it too in the circumstances. Pegg the Quaker was a worthy successor to Billingsley, John Brewer to Banford (for like Banford he was almost equally good at figure subjects, flowers, birds, fruit and landscapes). His brother Robert Brewer became the chief landscape painter, and so on.

In fact in 1795-1796 there was practically a peaceful revolution in the Derby Factory, and this date is an important one for Collectors to bear in mind.—For not only was there a change in the artistic side of the manufacture, but there occurred also a corresponding alteration in the manufacturing branch. The paste became harder and whiter, with a greenish translucency. The glaze became thinner and harder—the painting more on the surface—less absorbed in the glaze—the gilding, too, thinner, for the glaze would not hold the thick honey gold so lavishly and artistically put on by Soar and Stables. The discipline too, so strongly inculcated by Duesbury II, was allowed to become lax.

As Wm. Duesbury III grew up family troubles arose between him and his stepfather. Duesbury III never seems to have taken any prominent part in the Management of the Factory, but seldom went through the workshops and left no personal impression on the business.

In 1811, when Duesbury III was twenty-four years old, and had married three years before the daughter of a London Customer named Wm. E. Sheffield, Kean retired from the concern in disgust, and Sheffield buying his interest in it, the firm became for a time Duesbury & Sheffield. Kean died in 1823.

Kean having retired, there appears to have been no one very capable of carrying on the business. Duesbury III was unfitted by temperament, Sheffield by age and antecedents. Consequently it went rapidly down hill, and in 1815, four years after Kean's retirement, Duesbury III was glad to get the business off his hands by leasing it to Robert Bloor, the book-keeper, who had for some time looked after the commercial side.

Robert Bloor faced a bad time with considerable courage. It was just after the battle of Waterloo had ended the long Napoleonic wars. All the nations were exhausted, taxes and wages were high, labour scarce and insubordinate; yet, assisted by his brother Joseph, Robert Bloor, not then a young man, took on the tottering business and saved it, nay restored it to much of its old prosperity and artistic excellence. Drastic measures were necessary.

Writers who do not realise the conditions of commercial England at the end of the Napoleonic wars blame Bloor for Derby Porcelain's artistic decadence. Rather should he receive a mead of praise. He took the vast stores of white undecorated porcelain, which had accumulated during the bad times of the war, from the storehouses, good and bad, firsts, seconds, thirds, as they came; decorated them with the bright, popular Japan and similar patterns, and sold them for what they would fetch in auctions all over the country and abroad. Yes, for the moment he cheapened Derby Porcelain and made it common; but this was only an emergency measure and immediately justified itself. He quickly realised large sums of money. He paid off the Duesbury family and acquired sole control of the business. He put the concern safely and soundly on its feet again, and then he turned to the artistic side and did his utmost to restore the ancient glories of Derby porcelain. Good artist-workmen were engaged and encouraged to do their best, men like Thos. Steele, the finest fruit painter of his day, the Hancocks, Moses Webster, an excellent flower painter, Lucas less successful with landscapes, Dodson with birds, all give the Connoiseur of this day, a century afterwards, something to admire even in Bloor China.

Services were made for Royalty and for the nobility.

The public taste of that period was of course at a low ebb, and undoubtedly Bloor had to cater for his public.

The strain, however, of this struggle, successful as it was, had been too much for Robert Bloor; in 1828 he became insane and the factory was carried on for him by his Manager Thomason. In 1845 Robert Bloor died, followed a year later by his brother. After his death Thos. Clarke (who had married his granddaughter) tried to carry on the factory; but knowing nothing about the business he found it best to close it down gradually, and it ceased work entirely in 1848; the models, including most of those of the old Chelsea and Bow factories being sold to Samuel Boyle of Fenton, who in turn sold them to Copelands, in whose factory they have been disinterred recently by Mr Frank Stoner and exhibited and described by him to the joy of present-day Collectors.

Thus came to an end the Old Derby Factory

of Wm. Duesbury. But the manufacture of porcelain of good quality and artistic appearance is still carried on in the town of Derby, and shows every likelihood of so continuing.

Before ending this chapter a word may be said with advantage of its more exclusive productions. Those, that is, which differentiate its wares from those of any of its contemporaries.

First of all then come its figures, and especially its biscuit figures, *i.e.*, plain unglazed white figures.

These were a speciality of the Derby Factory and exceed both in quality, artistic merit, and number, those of any other factory at home or abroad.

Secondly, its blue ground colour. Up to 1782 Smith's blue, so called because it was invented or discovered by an employee named Smith, a brilliant semi-matt enamel blue, called at the factory and in the old sale catalogues the Lapis-lazuli blue was used. This was neither known nor used at any other factory whatever, and only at Derby (and Chelsea under Duesbury) till the year 1782.

In the same year 1782 that the new fine underglaze cobalt blue ground was invented and introduced at Derby, the crossed batons and dots were added to the Crown and D. mark.

This fact is of immense importance in fixing the date of any Derby piece and also in identifying unmarked Derby or Chelsea Derby pieces.

Thirdly, Derby was the first factory to introduce the painting of flowers and landscapes in a natural as opposed to a conventional manner—Billingsley introduced the one, John and Robert Brewer the other.

Fourthly, a Derby man (Hancock) discovered, and Derby popularised, the brown burnished or mercury gold, which has superseded the beautiful old honey gold.

A word may also be said about the earlier productions of Derby. As far as is known these, before the year 1769-1770, bore no distinguishing marks whatever. It was apparently owing to his then buying the Chelsea Factory and so the need of distinguishing between the two factories' productions that induced Duesbury to adopt the Crown and *D* mark.

The Author believes that at least half the unmarked figures and vases, sauceboats, and other pieces attributed in these days to Chelsea, were actually made at Derby. If not, where are they? The wares made in great quantity between 1756 and 1770 by a factory so prosperous and successful that it absorbed Chelsea, Bow, Lambeth, and Giles's business cannot have vanished into thin air, or even all have been lost or broken.

The British Museum and the Victoria and Albert Museum each possesses a small white glazed moulded Cream Jug resembling the famous 1745 Goat and Bee Jugs of Chelsea in shape and paste, but modelled with strawberry leaves and fruit, each of which has a large incised D under the base. An example is illustrated here from the V. and A. Museum by kind permission of the Authorities.

In the Author's opinion these Jugs are the earliest known examples of Derby porcelain, and were made by Butt Rivett & Heath at the Cockpit Hill Factory. Unless the small group of white glazed lambs, also illustrated here—which is marked under the base with an incised quinquangle ⬠ are the work of Andrew Planché fired in the pipekiln about 1745.

He would, however, direct investigators'

attention to certain points which may indicate a difference between true Chelsea figures and those which may possibly be attributed to Derby :—

(*a*) The colour of the pink or puce on the garments. The same colour was used on both; but owing to the different nature of the two pastes or bodies, on the Chelsea figures it assumed a colder more purple pink—on the Derby a rosier warmer pink.

(*b*) The painting of the flower sprays on the garments or robes of figures—on the Derby figures this often consists of plain maroon or crimson flowers on a pale yellow ground.

(*c*) The modelled flowers on base and bocage show a difference.

(*d*) Figures of the same or similar models (the two factories copied each other's figures, as also did Bow), where one is marked with the Anchor of Chelsea and the other is not, should be carefully compared for these differences.

It has often been a matter of surprise that Duesbury I, a man with such an eye for the main chance, never exploited the immense possibilities of the blue and white tea and coffee ware trade, in imitation of the then popular Nankin article, as carried on at Worcester and Bow. Various reasons are given by writers, mostly erroneous.

Duesbury I did try and, like everything else he did, he tried hard. He even got Richard Holdship of Worcester to come and show him the way; but he failed for two reasons:—

(1) The Derby body would not stand boiling water without cracking.

(2) The Derby glaze was too soft for the underglaze painted or printed cobalt blue; the colour invariably ran.

The only blue that would not run with Duesbury I's glaze was Smith's blue, and though this was tried (see accompanying rare illustration of a blue and white, marked, handleless cup in the Author's possession), instead of the glaze running bright and true over it, it showed matt and dull through the glaze.

But it is not generally known that Duesbury I did try to meet the Worcester and Bow competition by importing blue and white Nankin ware, and often added, as he thought, to its attractiveness by adding gilded lines and ornament to its decoration.

Most of the blue and white Nankin so gilded was thus decorated at Derby. Sometimes a small gold D will be found inside the bottom rim of the teapot; sometimes a gilder's number.

The study of Old Derby Porcelain will bring to the Collector's mind one outstanding characteristic, individuality; and it is this feature that the following chapters are intended to make clear.

Studied on these lines there is no porcelain in the world which will appeal more to the appreciation and even to the affection of a lover of old china.

CHAPTER II

The Modellers and Figure-Makers of Old Derby Porcelain

from these, and when hard enough to handle, the repairers joined them together and set them on a base with the necessary slip or jointing material; afterwards, when set, smoothing off the rough parts of the joints with a knife or brush, sharpening up the moulding where necessary and under-cutting.

It would, therefore, be more likely that the repairer or moulder would impress his initial letter on the piece, or even in the case of pieces made to order, put on the initial letter of the customer to distinguish the piece when it came out of the oven or enamelling kiln. Several records that have come down to us point to one or other of these explanations being the true one of the impressed letters found under the base of statuettes and figures.

For instance we know that though Spängler modelled the famous groups after Bartolozzi's prints of Angelica Kauffmann's paintings:—No. 195—The Awakening of Cupid; No. 196—Two Bacchante Decorating the Bust of Pan; and No. 235—Three Virgins Distressing Cupid. These never bear the signature of Spängler or even an S indicating his initial, but the marks of the repairers, *i.e.*, a triangle for Joseph Hill, a star for Isaac Farnsworth, or a W for Whittaker. It is true that Stephan on rare occasions inscribed his name on the base of a figure; but as his agreement of 17th September, 1770, with Wm. Duesbury shows, he was engaged to both model *and repair* china or porcelain ware at a wage of £2 12s. 6d. a week. It is true also that Spängler was also bound by his agreement of 13th September, 1790, to "himself make an original in porcelain from each of the models" and may possibly therefore have marked his name or initials on this "proof" figure of each of his models. On the other hand Spängler, who was notorious for not fulfilling his agreements, may not have carried out this part of his bargain. Certain it is that Spängler's name or initial is never found on a figure so far as is known at present.

During the early years of the Derby Factory Duesbury was content to more or less copy the models of Chelsea or Bow (curiously enough considering his connection with the Longton Hall Factory, we do not find distinctively Longton Hall figures reproduced at Derby); though even gilded cage and escapes. Alas, he is recaptured and brought back, no longer to a gilded cage even, but to iron bars. Only at the death of his captor does he finally get away—and then it is to freedom indeed, but poverty and distress—the end.

Spängler was a Swiss of German parentage, brought up to his art of modelling at the Zurich Factory by his father, one of the chief workmen from the Höchst Factory, who had brought the secrets of making hard paste porcelain to the newly started Zurich Factory. He appears to have come to London at the invitation of Mr Bn. Vulliamy, a noted clockmaker in London, and himself apparently a Swiss from Geneva. Vulliamy was fond of ornamenting his clocks with figures in marble or porcelain. These he may have got originally from Zurich; but becoming known to Lygo, Duesbury's very clever and energetic agent in London, the latter induced him to adopt the beautiful Derby biscuit figures for the purpose.

Soon he must have special figures—" Astronomy," " Æsculapius," &c. Duesbury has no one capable of modelling these now Stephan has left, so Spängler is introduced by Vulliamy, models these figures (and others) for Duesbury in London, charging big prices, for he only works when in the mood, and the rest of his time is passed in riotous living—the artistic temperament in fact. For " Astronomy " he gets ten guineas, and two and a half more for finishing it off properly later. Little work is turned out and that very expensive. Customers are kept waiting and are disappointed. What is to be done. Vulliamy and Duesbury put their heads together. Spängler shall be persuaded to go and work at the Derby Factory on a three years' agreement. He will be out of the temptations and attractions of the big city. Accordingly a temporary agreement is made 13th July, 1790. Spängler is to be paid for his models according to the time spent on them at the rate of three guineas a week (a very high rate for those days), he is to work shorter hours than others. His expenses are to be paid to Derby by coach. After a month's trial, if the parties like each other a proper agreement is to be made for a fixed time at two pounds ten shillings per week. This agreement is witnessed by Vulliamy. Presumably the arrangement was satisfactory to Spängler if it was not altogether so to Duesbury, for a formal agreement is drawn up, and after Spängler had gone up to London, chiefly at Duesbury's expense, to have it translated to him and examined (probably by Vulliamy), it is duly signed, apparently in London, for Vulliamy and Lygo witness it.

This agreement is dated 13th September, 1790, though it was evidently signed a few days later, and binds Spängler to work for Duesbury at Derby, or elsewhere at Duesbury's option, for three years at his own lodgings, open to Duesbury's inspection, ten hours a day in summer and eight hours a day in winter, and to be paid for the models executed, at the rate of two guineas per week and overtime at the same rate.

The agreement, which is very long and full of detail, is given in extenso by Bemrose. Wm. Duesbury was a very hard man, but he was also a very just man. He always liked to have everything cut and dried, all down in black and white. He then kept absolutely to the agreement himself and expected the other party to it to do likewise, which nine times out of every ten his workmen never did.

Probably the last thing Spängler intended was to abide by it. Soon he was at his old game. He began fairly well for him, turning out models for a pair of Figures with Vases, representing "Morning" and "Noon." These nevertheless he took apparently seven weeks to finish, for they cost Duesbury fourteen guineas the pair. The Three Graces took three weeks and cost six guineas, and so on.

Before very long, however, Spängler was in hot water with his employer through his idleness, neglect of work, breaches of contract and getting into debt. To pay these latter Duesbury lent him in 1792 thirty pounds on a bill of sale on his household effects. With this money in his pocket he promptly shook off the dust of the town from his feet and left Derby, probably not unaccompanied, for we read that he was captured at Ramsgate, and put into the King's Bench prison, probably at the instance of Duesbury. After he had had time to cool his heels there for a while, and as Duesbury thought had had time for consideration, he was bailed out by a friend and compatriot, one Hurter, on condition that he returned to Duesbury and worked off the debt. On this Duesbury made a new and far severer agreement with him, seeing that he had lost so much money over the last.

In this new agreement Spängler was to work at the same rate, but Duesbury was to deduct two thirds each week towards repayment of his debt and expenses until the amount was cleared off, and if Spängler lost more than half a day a week, Duesbury was to deduct 7/- a day from the remainder. Thus at the best poor Jean Jacques would only have 14/- a week left, and at the worst still less.

Under these circumstances the inevitable was not long in happening; by November of the same year he had absconded again and was back in London, this time arriving not by coach and four but on foot and sore.

Nothing, however, shows more clearly the irresponsible, impish character of the man than his treatment of his friend and benefactor Hurter, who at considerable risk and expense to himself had bailed him out of the King's Bench and gone surety for him. "On September the

9th," writes Hurter to Duesbury, " Spängler wrote me that he was working indefatigably " (how the rogue must have enjoyed the joke as he wrote it) " to bring under the ' pretended debt ' (as he called it);——but how great was my astonishment when last Saturday Sen' night I saw him arrive in the most pity full condition." (*sic*).

He told Hurter in reply to anxious enquiries as to whether the debt was discharged that he would hear no more of the debt and " without saying any more he sat down to dinner with me, and after dinner he went up into my room to shave himself and dress his hair; a little while after, my servant going up to make my bed found him in it. She told him he could not remain in the house, all the rooms being engaged. He begged to be left to take a little rest (being very ill) and he would rise again. I good-naturedly never intended to disturb him, and thought him really asleep in my room! 'till eleven o'clock when I went up to take a few things I wanted I found he was gone, and on looking round I missed several things which he has made free with to the amount of £4 4/-.

" Notwithstanding this I think he is still in London or its vicinity, and that he will have impudence enough to call on me or to write. However I give up every thought of making any good of him. Therefore must beg of you to dispose to the best advantage of those things he left in your possession and to let me know what further sum is coming to you without any more law proceedings." What could be done with such a character? And yet as one can see through all, Hurter loved the scamp. Duesbury too forgave him again, after receiving from him a most pitiful and penitent letter, and Spängler continues to do work for him in London. But this turns out utterly hopeless. No work, or scarcely any, is done, and so 1795 sees Spängler once more in Derby with an even stiffer agreement. True, under this he is to have his freedom, for a month's notice on either side is to terminate the agreement subject to finishing any model on hand. It is stated that Duesbury having been a great loser by Spängler under a former agreement shall have liberty to pay by day work or piecework at his option at the rate of four shillings per day of ten hours or by the piece,

ranging from pieces four inches to five inches high at 6/6, to pieces thirteen inches to fourteen inches high at 33/- and so on in proportion. In a letter dated 3rd February, 1795, Lygo says :—
" Spängler will set off for Derby to-morrow, he intends walking as it will not be so expensive, and he may as well be walking to Derby as stay here doing nothing."

So the naughty Jean Jacques is back again and works at Derby (or pretends to do so) till Duesbury II's death a year afterwards. When off he goes again. There is only one more record of him available, and that is in the recollections of old Isaac Farnsworth, who had moulded and " repaired " so many of his figures and groups, who afterwards became a foreman in the Derby factory, and who had no doubt had much trouble to get his models from the lazy Jean Jacques. He tells Haslem that shortly after leaving Derby Spängler passed through the town on tramp, dressed in the cast-off clothes of a soldier—were they indeed cast-off, or had naughty Jean Jacques made free with them as he did with Hurter's bed and belongings? If one knows one's Jean Jacques that too trusting soldier was bemoaning

Adonis !). Certainly the metamorphosed figure is a great success. The graceful pose, the Grecian features, the lifelike attitude of the dog, which seems, not without reason, to be trying to attract its master's attention, combine to make it a worthy companion to Stephan's Shepherdess. The original figure modelled in Dorset Clay and fired is in Nottingham Museum. This must have been one of the last figures modelled by Coffee before he left the Derby Factory for good, just as its Companion Shepherdess was probably Stephan's last effort there.

2. The Female Figure, No. 359, criticised by Lygo, is another, and

3. No. 378, Scotchman and Lass, the third.

In the Derby price-list of figures published by Haslem Nos. 335 to 359, twenty-five patterns, are described as " Spängler's and Coffee's Figures and Groups " with no further particulars. So that except for style one is unable to say which belongs to which.

This notice would not be complete without some mention of the early figure-makers (or repairers). The two principal of these were Joseph Hill and Isaac Farnsworth. The former marked the special figures which he made with a triangle incised in the soft clay, the latter with a star. However graceful and beautiful and true to nature a figure may be when it comes from the modeller's hands, it must be remembered that the model has to be cut up; each limb, the head, and sometimes part of the body being moulded or cast separately in Plaster of Paris moulds formed from the pieces of the model. These when sufficiently hard to handle have to be joined up with slips made of the same body and mounted on the appropriate base, with the dog, lamb, attributes, or flowers (also moulded separately), added in the same manner. Now a head can be put on the torso at many angles, or a limb in many positions, and the grace and pose of the figure all depend on this being done correctly. Also the joining-up marks and the division marks of the moulds have to be carefully smoothed or cut away and the whole to be gone over with tools to restore the folds in the draperies, &c.;

some having to be completely undercut, which is impossible to be effected by the moulds.

A great part of the success of a figure or group depends therefore on the work and skill of the repairer. Two collectors may each have a figure of a particular pattern number and model; but the two figures may vary vastly in gracefulness and naturalness of pose, in neatness of finish, and in the accessories. One in fact may be a beautiful and perfect work of art, the other may be stiff or malformed, anatomically incorrect and impossible, showing traces of joining up, and wanting in finish. Yet both may be from a model of Spängler.

The presence of a triangle or star incised under the base is usually a guarantee that the setting up and repairing of the figure is all that it should be. Of the two Joseph Hill was both the earlier and the finer figure-maker. He was one of Wm. Duesbury I's earliest apprentices and seems to have spent his whole working life at the Derby Factory.

Isaac Farnsworth came as an apprentice a year or two later and he also worked till his death, which occurred in 1821 or 1822, at the Derby

Factory. He was made foreman over the ornamental department, and as we have seen was a clever, kind hearted, hard-working man. Both Stephan's and Spängler's models were moulded and repaired by these two figure-makers.

Of the illustration of Spängler's famous groups after Bartolozzi's prints of Angelica Kauffmann's paintings, No. 195, "Cupid's Awakening," and No. 196, "The Adornment of Pan," both in the Author's Collection, the former is marked with the ⁂ of Isaac Farnsworth and the latter with the △ of Joseph Hill with an incised R in front, as if he meant to say "Repairer—Joseph Hill." The former is in the soft cream-coloured body, and the latter in the soft pure white translucent body with a soft gloss on it (not a glaze), which is believed to have been discovered during Kean's management.

These modellers were indeed fortunate in having two such artist-craftsmen as Hill and Farnsworth to interpret their beautiful models.

CHAPTER III

The Flower Painters on Old Derby Porcelain

CHAPTER III

The Flower Painters on Old Derby Porcelain.

In collecting old English porcelain, the work and individuality of the Painter whose work on this beautiful and fascinating medium gives the artistic and discriminating Collector so much pleasure is often forgotten or even ignored.

The same criticism applies in a great measure to the writers on English Ceramics.

This may be due to some extent to the lack of authentic information with regard to the early painters on China Ware. With regard to Chelsea porcelain, for instance, we know only a very few of the names of the later artists and still less are we able indubitably to identify their work. The same applies to Bow, Bristol, Lowestoft, Longton Hall, and Liverpool porcelain.

We know rather more of the old Worcester porcelain painters, though even so to a greater extent of the outside artists, such as Donaldson,

O'Neale, and Baxter, than the actual painters working at the factory itself, whether those trained in its decorating rooms or those who migrated from Chelsea, Bow, and other factories.

It is this partial lifting of the veil of ignorance and indifference from the work and personality of the old Derby porcelain painters which makes finely painted old Derby porcelain so entrancing and desirable to collectors.

Askew, Withers, Jockey Hill, Quaker Pegg, Duvivier, Boreman, Moses Webster, and William Billingsley, above all Billingsley (or Beeley as he sometimes called himself) among the painters, Spängler, Stephan, Rossi among the modellers, Hill and Farnsworth who made up their figures, Soar and Keys among the gilders, all live as human (often very human) beings in the entrancing pages of John Haslem's book ("The Old Derby China Factory") and endear themselves, their idiosyncrasies, and their living work to the collector of old porcelain.

We seem to see Jockey Hill galloping along the mean streets riding donkey-wise on the haunches of Bob his pony, with his coat tails flying behind him and the urchins at the street corners applauding. We think of Bob the pony going home by himself with the reins thrown over his shoulders and coming back equally on his own at " knocking-off time " for his master to ride home. And the vision and the thought make us see something of the kindly patient nature of the mutilated painter in his softly pencilled landscapes on the soft and translucent porcelain.

We envisage surely Wm. Pegg the Quaker, born with a love of flowers, for was he not the son of a gardener, loving first pleasure, forsaking her for Art. He writes in his Apologia vita sua—

" Then I broke my old connexions,
Placed on drawing my affections,
Dedicated all my powers
To the Arts in leisure hours,
Painting still engrossed my passion "—

and lastly forsaking even his beloved Art for his God, as he saw Him. Driven to hard monotonous unremunerative distasteful labour by his over tender conscience and stern, almost savage, self-mortification.

When we think of these things and look at this

glorious Moss Rose (Pl. 22), almost natural size, palpitating with life and colour, its tender translucent petals standing out from the plain undecorated plate, every hair of its moss, the very ravagement by insects of its leaves, portrayed with a loving conscientiousness only equalled by its skill, we feel that we know the painter by his work and his work by the character of the painter.

How, one may ask, can one know and recognise Quaker Pegg's work on old Derby porcelain?

In the old Derby pattern book the only patterns specifically directed to be painted by Pegg, according to Haslem, are :—No. 475, cup, "Flowers on warm olive ground in oval $2\frac{1}{4}$ inches by $1\frac{3}{4}$ inches, by Pegg," and No. 240, a plate, with five compartments in the border, in which are "Flowers, by Pegg"; but the collector, besides knowing Pegg's particular style from well authenticated pieces (see plates Nos. 21, 22, 57 and 58), will have noticed the following points in connection with Pegg's work which assist materially in forming a correct judgment in the matter.

The Flower Painters

1. Quaker Pegg only started work at the Old Derby Factory in 1796, the year Billingsley left. He was therefore probably engaged to take his place. This was also the year of Wm. Duesbury the Second's death. The porcelain would therefore be for the first period during which Pegg worked at Derby, *i.e.*, five years, glazed with the thinner, harder glaze of that period. During the latter period, 1810 to 1823, the glaze became again softer and thicker, also liable to craze. But during both periods the body was phosphatic, *i.e.*, it contained a considerable proportion of calcined bones, and had a green translucency when viewed by transmitted light.

2. The mark was, it is believed, invariably in red and consisted of the crown with batons and D rarely with DK (the D K or Duesbury & Kean mark).

   It has also been noticed that Quaker Pegg made his crown wide and flat and his crossed batons to match.

   The crown 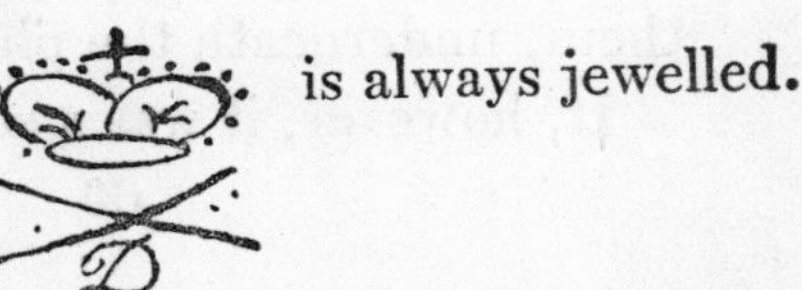 is always jewelled.

3. The use of the new opaque chrome green[5] can almost always be noticed in his leaves instead of the translucent copper green[6] seen on the work of the earlier painters.

4. The group of flowers, or even a single flower, was almost always painted nearly life size, much larger than the flowers painted by the other Derby flower painters, and would usually cover the whole of the available surface. For this reason there were scarcely ever any Arabesque borders or gilded design borders on pieces painted by Quaker Pegg. For the most part a broad or narrow band of gilding round the extreme edge of the plate was the only other ornament it had.

5. Although Pegg painted well and with extreme conscientiousness, he seems to have been doubtful whether people would always recognise his flowers for what they were intended to be; for he almost invariably wrote the name of the flowers in red paint opposite them, underneath the plate or other piece.

If, however, it was a single flower that was

with black, dark brown, or neutral colour, with a very fine pencil and in a most delicate manner, the greens being brushed over afterwards—the stalks are thin lines of colour. The flowers have the high lights left. One principal flower, such as a rose or poppy in a bunch or group of flowers, almost always sprays out beyond the others in a very graceful manner. This latter idiosyncracy was much copied by other painters at Derby, and became almost a "Derby manner." It was carried by them to Pinxton, Worcester, Nantgarw, Swansea, Coalport, and the nineteenth century Staffordshire factories; but it is not found on the older eighteenth century factories outside Derby. These followed the Meissen and Sèvres example, and if any flowers protruded from the group it was a spray of small flowers or florets.

It has already been stated that Withers was not steady in his habits, possibly what we should call in these days the artistic temperament. He seems to have lost his employment at Derby; becoming a rolling stone, working in Staffordshire, Birmingham, and London; finally he returned to Derby, where, after a short spell of employment, he died in great distress and was buried at the expense of his shopmates.

One name, one personality, however, stands out above all the Derby flower painters, possibly above all the workmen-artists employed at the various early English factories—William Billingsley.

Not perhaps altogether an exemplary character, his genius, his artistic skill and taste, his white-hot enthusiasm for his creative trade, his love of beauty, of perfection for itself, his power of absorption of all that was most perfect and beautiful around him, set him on a plane apart, with such names as Palissy and Dwight and Böttger. While his very misfortunes of humble birth, of early orphanage, of limited opportunities, of irrascible and overbearing temper, his impatience of opposition, his affection for others, and the affection and devotion he inspired in others, his very failure to perfect the manufacture in a commercial sense (in an artistic sense he reached a perfection which has never been surpassed, perhaps never can be surpassed) of his beautiful porcelain, all endear the man and his work to the artistic and appreciative collector.

This article, however, is not concerned with Billingsley as the creator of the most beautiful porcelain ever invented, but as the greatest of Old Derby Flower Painters.

It seems to have been Boreman, as he was called at Derby, who took the promising young Billingsley under his wing and taught him much of his trade. Probably Duvivier, another French or Flemish artist from Chelsea, working at Derby after the closing of the Chelsea Factory, helped to form his style, for all through his career Billingsley seems to have drawn his inspiration from France and Sèvres rather than from Meissen or the Orient. All the artistic impulses of the day seem to have been eagerly absorbed by this working lad, and out of it all he evolved his own inspirations, his own methods both of porcelain manufacture and porcelain painting which were to revolutionise the ceramic art and practice of his time.

Billingsley himself thought but little of his flower painting as compared with his porcelain, the former was but a means to the latter, it brought in the money which he squandered without thought of personal advantage, wife or children, home or rest, on his beloved porcelain.

Yet it is by his flower painting on porcelain that his reputation was made, and it is by his flower painting on porcelain that his fame will continue.

For one collector who treasures Billingsley's porcelain there are a hundred who love his flower painting, and perhaps there are a thousand who admire and collect what they fondly imagine is Billingsley's work, but which is really work done in his style and after his manner by his pupils, his disciples, and last, but not least, by his imitators.

For one genuine piece painted by Billingsley there are a thousand or more painted in Billingsley's style. Most of his genuine work was done at Derby where he worked over twenty years, and is therefore on Derby porcelain of body glaze and marks that show it to have been made and decorated before 1795-1796, the date at which he left Derby. At that date when Mr Lygo, Wm. Duesbury's London Agent, heard that Billingsley was leaving Derby, he wrote to his employer :—" I hope you will be able to make a bargain with Mr Billingsley for him to continue with you, for it will be a great loss to lose such a hand, and not only that, but his going to another factory will put them in the way of doing flowers in the same way, which at present they are entirely ignorant of." Lygo's misgivings were amply fulfilled.

Bemrose writes :—" In our days there is much of the flower painting attributed to Billingsley by collectors and dealers, and exhibited under his name in the museums, that is not worthy of his brush. His painting has a fatty, soft-glaze look when compared with that of his contemporaries; his grouping is good, and he often throws out from bouquets long delicately-painted sprays. He also painted his flowers in truer perspective by an effective treatment of shadows; his colouring is more delicate than that of most other artists, he was fond of yellow and puce, and often introduced white flowers. His leaves are generally dark and but slightly veined and outlined, and are painted with greater freedom and want of detail when compared with his flowers."

Haslem adds his testimony thus:—"It is remarkable that there is so little old china to be met with painted with flowers in the unmistakeable style which Billingsley practised before he left Derby.—After he left Derby his style was simply of a commonplace decorative character and nearly destitute of the artistic excellence of his earlier flower painting. Doubtless Billingsley's time was so much occupied by the general management of the concerns while at Pinxton, Mansfield, and Nantgarw that he had a very little time to spare for painting at those places."

We give as frontispiece and in our plates an illustration of possibly the finest authentic example in existence of Billingsley's flower painting, executed at the Derby Factory about 1792-1795, the zenith of his powers as a painter.

This is a Toilet Ewer and Basin suitable for fitting in one of the square Chippendale or Hepplewhite wash-hand stands of the time, having a hole in the centre into which the basin fitted. This is in the collection of the Author.

The large size and available surface of these pieces of exquisite Old Derby porcelain have given Billingsley an opportunity of putting out his full powers such as he can seldom have had, and he has accordingly taken full advantage of it. The pencilling and colour scheme are of the boldest character, yet executed with perfect finish. Compare the construction of the groups of flowers (all his favourites, pink moss roses, passion flower, Iris, spikes of yellow hollyhock, and masses of puce flowers, with spreading, delicately painted sprays amongst them) with Bemrose's description of Billingsley's style. Note the dark less finely finished leaves, the perspective skilfully effected by the shadows, and compare this with the beautifully pencilled but flat appearance of Pegg's, Wither's, and Moses Webster's flowers. These pieces show Billingsley's true Derby style and are a touchstone to which all other examples can be brought.

These wonderful pieces are of Derby porcelain and are translucent. The body and glaze[8] are soft and limpid with a creamy translucency. They have rich and handsome borders executed by Thomas Soare (or Soar) in thick soft honey-gold and colours. Thos. Soar was one of William Duesbury's oldest hands, a fine painter of

Arabesques and gilder, and his number was 1, being foreman over the painting rooms.

The mark is in puce on both pieces, as under :—

Now on looking up the record of the Old Derby pattern book one finds pattern No. 172, " A group by Billensley in centre with a rich border in colours and gold."

Apart from its artistic qualities, Billingsley's work on Derby porcelain may be traced by bearing in mind the following considerations :—

1. He worked at Derby under Wm. Duesbury the first, 1774-1786, und Wm. Duesbury the second, 1786-1796; but it must be remembered that during a large part of the first Wm. Duesbury's proprietorship he was only an apprentice and would be employed on painting simple borders and designs on the

cheaper services. Keys in his account says that an order having come in for some china "to match a Chelsea plate with a single plant in a curious style from nature," and Withers the best flower painter having just left, it was doubtful whether the order could be executed. However, Billingsley made the attempt with the instructions of Mr Boreman. He copied any garden or wild flowers that suited, and when the order was sent off it gave great satisfaction. It also gave Billingsley his chance to show what he could do and from that time Duesbury made him his principal flower painter.

Now we have seen that Withers left the Derby Factory about 1790 and Billingsley also left in 1795 or very early in 1796. All Billingsley's work of any consequence therefore on Derby porcelain must have been done in the five or six years between 1790 and 1795. Before that he would be executing small flowers on services, putting in minute flowers in the basket or wreath of Askew's or Banford's Cherubs, in accordance with the subdivision of labour which was the rule under the elder Duesbury. Even during this comparatively short period of five and a half years, we know from the notes in the Old Derby pattern book that the greater part of Billingsley's time was occupied in painting the small stereotyped flowers in the conventional patterns of that period, as for instance in the cornucopia pattern No. 174 and the conventional rose and cornflower pattern eight times repeated round the border of a plate as pattern No. 53. Even the charming rose and lily of the valley pattern round the border of plate pattern No. 176, so reminiscent of the Prentice Plate, while it shows Billingsley's charm and method, hardly affords scope for his special gifts of light and shadow, grouping, colouring, and perspective.

If one appreciates the considerations set forth above, one can hardly share John Haslem's wonder that so few authentic and recognised specimens of Billingsley's painting on Old Derby porcelain remain to us, or that really choice specimens of his Derby work are so rare.

2. Old Derby pieces painted by Wm. Billingsley with flowers of any consequence therefore would be made between 1790 and 1795. They should have a creamy translucency, soft paste,[9] and soft thick limpid glaze. They would be marked with the crowned D, with crossed batons, and almost always in puce, the mark being carefully drawn and the crown symmetrically jewelled.

It has been said, and repeated without verification by succeeding writers, that the number 7 on an Old Derby piece indicates that it was painted by Billingsley. Haslem, however, writes:—"The gilders also had marks but did not use them so often, most, if not the whole of the names opposite the numbers given, with the exception of Billingsley were gilders; and if he ever used the number (7) attributed to him, it must have been rarely, as he (John Haslem) has not found it on more than one genuine example of his work; but he has met with the number 7 on several specimens of Derby china of that period into the decoration of which flowers did not enter."

With this conclusion the Author is in agreement.

3. The following patterns in the Old Derby pattern books are marked to be done by Billensley (as Duesbury always wrote his name) :—

No. 53. Roses and Cornflowers by Billensley.

No. 135. Moses (Mosses?) with some tinging (hanging?) yellow flowers upon a faint brown shaded ground by Billensley.

No. 144. A group of coloured flowers by Billensley.

No. 172. A group by Billensley in centre with a rich border in colours and gold. (See frontispiece and plates Nos. 19 and 20.

No. 174. Cornucopias, fruit and flowers by Billensley.

No. 176. A rich border of roses and lilys of the valley, bell shaped sprigs in centre by Billensley.

No. 180. Cupid painted by Askew, flowers, basket, clouds, &c., by Billensley.

No. 246. Teacup, fawn coloured, Vandyke border, painted blue leaved Coronilla plant by Billensley.

No. 326. Basket of flowers upon pedistall before olive ground by Billensley.

No. 351. Mug, ground of flowers by Billensley, filled in with gold, with subject in a compartment, " Cupid disarmed " by Banford.

This is the last time Billingsley's name occurs in these pattern books.

No doubt other patterns may have been painted by Billingsley; but these are the only ones which we can say definitely were painted by him, and then only if the paste, glaze, style, and marks of the period 1790-1795 agree, for many of the same patterns were doubtless painted before and after he left the factory by other painters.

4. The flowers must be painted by the wiping out process, the leaves will have the opaque chrome green visible, often with a touch of orange brown. The grouping will be artistic, and the modelling rounded and in perspective.

5. As Billingsley's painting at this period was much esteemed and his work in great request, it would only appear as a rule on the more elaborate and costly services, &c. It would therefore generally be accompanied by fine thick gilding and often by ground colours and rich borders. The gilding would always be of the soft honey gold, as Hancock only discovered the mercury gold about 1800.

Billingsley died in January, 1828, at the age of 69 at Coalport, where he had been employed by Mr John Rose, the proprietor, since leaving Nantgarw for the last time in 1819, as foreman. In the Author's opinion, Billingsley did no painting on porcelain at Nantgarw, Swansea, or

Coalport. He has met with Billingsley's very distinctive painting on Derby, Pinxton, and Worcester porcelain (see plate No. 8); but not on any other.

All the Nantgarw, Swansea, and Coalport specimens attributed to Billingsley, have been painted by Pardoe, Pollard, Pegg the younger, and Morris.

A fourth Old Derby ceramic artist who painted long and painted well was Moses Webster. This painter served his apprenticeship at the Old Derby Factory; but on coming out of his time, joined a china decorating shop in London, run by Robins & Randall, where he is believed to have decorated some of the earlier Nantgarw porcelain—thence he went to the Worcester Factory, and is said to have received instruction in painting from Thos. Baxter in the latter's School of Art there, returning to paint at Derby Factory about 1816—leaving to take up John Keys' connection as a Drawing Master in the town on the latter's death in 1825.

Haslem says that his work on Derby is scarce, that his flowers have a somewhat dashed and faded appearance as if they had been kept in water too long; but that notwithstanding this peculiarity he was one of the best of the later Derby painters; that his groups are tastefully arranged and that there is a dash and freedom in his execution.

He was born in 1792 and died at the age of 78 years in 1870.

His best known work, and perhaps his finest, was on the service made at the Derby Factory for Mr John Trotter of Durham Park about 1820, and the plate illustrated (Fig. 25) is a piece of this service. It has Mr Trotter's name and place written on the back, with a carefully drawn crown, crossed batons and D underneath. All in gold.

The five dark panels are of chrome green. The flowers are beautifully painted and are skilfully arranged to form a completely circular decoration in the centre of the plate. This group, as can be seen from the illustration, exactly conforms to Haslem's description of Webster's work; but what the illustration does not show is, that the colours used give the flowers just that dashed and faded look of having been kept too long in water that Haslem described.

One need say little more, then, to enable one to distinguish Webster's work on Derby porcelain. It will usually be on the creamy ground and thickish glaze that came into vogue about 1810.

It will have the Derby marks of the Robert Bloor period, for none of his painting, as an apprentice, would either be recognisable or worth collecting, being chiefly borders and trade patterns.

But one thing will always be found in Moses Webster's later work—it will always be well and carefully done, and it will always be charming.

Others among the Old Derby flower painters[10] are Fidèle Duvivier, whose paintings though they must be fairly numerous have not yet been definitely identified. The other Wm. Pegg, James Turner, Leonard Lead, John Stanesby, and others, all worked in a very similar manner without any outstanding characteristics to distinguish their work. These do not therefore appeal to the collector in the same way that a piece beautifully painted by Billingsley, Pegg, Withers, or even Webster does. Of course there were other artists at Derby, hardly, if any, less interesting, or their work less desirable, than these; Askew, Banford, Robert Brewer, are all names to charm with; Banford especially has never yet had full justice done to his beautiful and versatile work or his interesting character and career. But these were figure or landscape painters and theirs is another story, which is told in the following and preceding chapters.

CHAPTER IV

THE FIGURE-SUBJECT PAINTERS ON OLD DERBY PORCELAIN

CHAPTER IV

THE FIGURE-SUBJECT PAINTERS ON OLD DERBY PORCELAIN.

UNDOUBTEDLY the best of the early Derby figure-subject painters was Richard Askew. He was a painter of figure subjects at Chelsea under Sprimont, chiefly of Cupids in rose colour or crimson. These he painted in a most charming style, free, bold, and natural, full of life and movement and no two alike. It is almost certain that he made drawings of these from his own infant children. They are real. They are lifelike. They are not copied from the cherubs in mediæval pictures or from the Cupids of Bartolozzi, Cipriana, Angelica Kauffmann, Strong, or the French artists Bourcher, Fragonard, or their school. They are what might well be described as native English Cupids and a credit to the country of their origin.

This only applies to Askew's manner of painting; the form of decoration consisting of

Cupids executed in pink camaieu is of course taken from the Vincennes, Sèvres, and other early soft-paste French factories, a style of decoration that was copied in all the European factories at that period.

We find these charming Cupids in pink camaieu of Askew on fine Chelsea vases of the later Sprimont period, on cups and saucers with yellow ground such as those advertised to be sold by Mr Christie in December, 1766, mentioned by Nightingale.

Later on we see them on beautiful richly decorated Chelsea-Derby services in the Sèvres manner; but these are rare, for Askew only worked one year, or at most two years, at Chelsea under Duesbury's auspices. That was in 1770-1772. In the latter year William Duesbury induced him to come to the Derby Factory.

When Duesbury first started at the Derby China Factory he turned his main attention to figures (images as they were quaintly called), also to useful articles, services, &c. Such vases as were made were decorated with flowers, in the Dresden manner, and sometimes with birds. Figure subjects were almost unknown. Duesbury, himself an expert enameller who had carried on an enamelling business for the china trade in London for several years, was capable of putting his painters in the way of all the enamelling described above, but when it came to painting figure subjects this was a matter beyond his powers and experience.

When he acquired the Chelsea Works he apparently carried it on only in a small way. Four painters, Boreman, Wollams (probably Williams), Snowden, and Jinks doing all the ordinary decorating; *vide* the weekly bills made out by Richard Barton the foreman, in 1770-1771, given by Jewitt—Askew's name does not appear in this list, though Jewitt says his name appears in some of the weekly bills.

Duesbury apparently argued that he could get any Chelsea-Derby pieces decorated with figure subjects in London by the expert trade enamellers; but his Derby pieces could hardly be sent up to London safely and profitably for this purpose.

It would be better to get Mahomet down to the mountain rather than transport the mountain to Mahomet. In 1771 or 1772, therefore, he agreed with Richard Askew to come down to Derby and do his figure subjects there.

Henceforth we find Askew's beautiful Cupids on Derby porcelain, and as he was the only figure painter at that date he not only painted Cupids en camaieu but in colours, and other figure subjects in colours. At Chelsea Askew's pay was at the rate of 4/2 per day; but at Derby it was raised to 5/3 per day, though apparently he was always paid by the piece, but reckoned the time taken over a piece at that rate. Thus a coffee can, painted with a portrait of the King of France, took one day and was charged 5/3; but a coffee can, painted with "a man and woman offering to Cupid," took three and a half days and cost 18/4 for the painting. While four coffee cans, painted with the four elements, took four days each and cost £4 4/-. In addition he was paid at about the same rate for drawing subjects—thus "three weeks drawing of Cupids, £4 14/6." This was in 1794.

From the fact that Askew's name never appears in lists of the regular painters at the factory either at Chelsea or Derby, it would appear that he always worked outside the factory

—probably latterly at his own home in Birmingham.

In his 1794 agreement with Duesbury he is described as "enamel painter of Birmingham" and as living at 8 Friday Street, Birmingham. In this agreement it is set out that his work must be "in quality and effect equal to the Cupids on two flower pots by James Banford." This does not mean that the latter was the better painter, but that Askew being paid by the piece had been scamping his work—now, he was put on his metal with a touch of professional jealousy.

How may Askew's painting be recognised :—

1. We find that Richard Askew began work at the Derby Factory about the end of 1771 or beginning of 1772. His work on Derby porcelain would therefore be on porcelain with the early body and glaze, soft paste with creamy translucency and thick pellucid glaze. Most of his Derby work would be marked with the D surmounted with a jewelled crown *without* crossed batons.

   The actual time of his ceasing to paint for the Derby Factory we do not know, nor yet the date of his death. All we do know is that he was painting for Duesbury in 1795, as we have his piecework accounts for work done in that year. Richard Askew's last account for piecework was paid in 1795. Billingsley was trying to leave in 1795 and actually did leave either at the end of that year or early in 1796. Jas. Banford too left in 1795. At that date Wm. Duesbury the second was ill and dying, and did die in 1796. Feeling his inability to carry on the business without help he took Michael Kean, a miniature painter, into partnership. What more likely than that these old hands and able painters disliked having Kean put over them and accordingly determined to leave.

The last two patterns mentioned in the Old Derby pattern book as being painted by either of them are :—

No. 387. Coloured group by Banford.
No. 389. Venus and Cupid (in colours) by Askew.

After that the figure subject pieces are done by John Brewer, who we find was engaged to come and do work as a regular hand in 1795. No doubt he was engaged to take their place, as otherwise there would have been no painter of figure subjects at the Derby Factory—just as Quaker Pegg was taken on at the same time as a substitute for Billingsley in flower painting.

2. As already pointed out, Askew's original work was represented for the most part by his delightful paintings of Cupids in rose pink camaieu. These are less beautiful than natural and living-like.

They are usually depicted flying, sitting, or lying on their backs among the clouds in every conceivable attitude, and are drawn in with extraordinary sureness and vigour. The outlines are apparently drawn first and then the shadows filled in with broad washes of a fully charged brush, after the style of the old Delft and Majolica painters. There is no hatching or stippling or finishing, the whole thing is bold, assured, and individual.

Askew's painting of other subjects in colours lacks this quality of spontaneity and sureness.

These figure subjects are evidently copied, more or less carefully from pictures, miniatures and other originals. The drawing and colouring are usually good and there is more care in the finishing.

3. The marks would be on Derby porcelain

 in blue or puce—more rarely 

in blue, puce, or red; but more frequently Askew's work is not marked at all.

4. The patterns marked in the old pattern books to be done by him are (the original spelling is retained):—

No. 361. Love Sleeps.
No. 363. Figure in colours.
No. 374. A Board (" Aboard ") in colours.
No. 389. Venus and Cupid (in colours).
No. 177. Cupid on a basket of flowers in the clouds.
No. 180. Cupit, painted by Askew ; flowers basket, clouds, &c., by Billensley.

He also did a few landscapes on services, &c.

Richard Askew had a son Robert Askew, whom he brought with him to Derby (or Birmingham) in 1772 and who was either apprenticed, or engaged to Wm. Duesbury at the Derby Factory. Robert, however, did not like the work, so he absconded the same year with John Laurence, another young hand, and was advertised in the Birmingham newspapers. John Laurence went to London where he worked in Wedgwood's Chelsea Decorating Establishment. Possibly Robert Askew did the same.

Askew's paintings on vases especially, but also on cabinet and caudle cups, &c., are highly esteemed by collectors and obtain high prices.

The second Old Derby figure painter was James Banford. He too was an old Chelsea painter and was induced by Duesbury to come to Derby.

He was a very clever painter and could paint not only figure subjects but also birds, flowers, and landscapes. He did as a matter of fact do all four at Derby; but it is as a painter of figure subjects that his fame endures.

Banford's work is much less bold and original, less full of life and motion than Askew's; but it is on the other hand much more carefully painted and more miniature-like. His colouring is always harmonious and restrained, and his paintings have a finished appearance.

Unfortunately he was much too fond of his glass, and was quarrelsome and touchy.

When his master, Duesbury, utilized his diverse talents by putting him on to landscapes or flowers he protested that he was not a chameleon to change his colours, and complained that he was not paid as high wages as Boreman, who, except for landscapes, he considered his inferior.

Had it not been that he had a most devoted and hard-working wife, Bernice, who worked all her spare time at home painting patterns, and thus managed to keep a roof over their heads, he would have come to grief much sooner than he did.

Poor Bernice. Jewitt gives in full two of her pathetic letters to Duesbury, one asking for work by the piece at the minimum rate of a guinea and a half for the first year and two guineas per week afterwards.

Apparently, like Askew, he painted at home, for his name does not appear in the lists of workmen at the Factory, nor was he required to mark his paintings with a number.

Jewitt in his first edition (Vol. II, p. 107) gives a list of his piece-time accounts from which the subjects he painted on Derby porcelain can be ascertained. These included such diverse subjects as among others :—

2 Coffee Cups and Stands, Shipping N.
6 Plates of Plants.
4 Comports of Landscapes.
2 Coffee Cans, Moonlight and Fire.
2 Coffee Cans and Stands, Birds.
2 Teapots Landscapes from Gilpin.
20 Plates of Rose Border.
2 Cabinet Cups, 1st and 2nd Lesson of Love.
4 Coffee Cans of Fowers.

In the Old Derby pattern books the following patterns are specially marked to be done by him :—

No. 391. Basket of Flowers in colours.

No. 393. Flora on one cup and a Muse on the other (in colours).

No. 414. A Bacchante (in colours), Adelaide (in colours) on the other can.

No. 415. Love Sleeps (in colours), Maid of Corinth (in colours) on the other can.

No. 432. Coloured Figures.

For the rest his work on Derby would

1. be on the harder porcelain with phosphatic body, thin glaze, and green translucency.
2. It would be marked with the D K mark for a very short time in red thus—

and afterwards with the usual jewelled crown, crossed batons and D mark in red.

3. His work would be finely and delicately done, but in the modern wipe-out style for flowers and high lights, the use of chrome green and mostly burnished mercury gold would be found on most of the articles painted by him.

The Figure-Subject Painters

It is not known how long John Brewer worked at Derby. Certainly he left before 1811 and set up as a Drawing Master in Derby. He soon got together a large clientele of pupils, which he succeeded in keeping till his death in the hour of England's great victory at Waterloo in 1815, for his brother Robert found it would pay him better to leave the factory and take up John Brewer's profession as a Drawing Master than remain on there.

A painting of Cupid in the Clouds on a fine Derby vase by John Brewer, illustrated here, gives a good idea of his style—it is done exactly like a miniature.

CHAPTER V

The Landscape Painters on Old Derby Porcelain

CHAPTER V

The Landscape Painters on Old Derby Porcelain

Landscape painting on porcelain, whether vases or still more plates and services generally, was a speciality of the Old Derby Porcelain Factory. It is true that we have beautiful miniature-like paintings of ports, seascapes, and hunting scenes on old Meissen porcelain. Conventional landscapes—mostly en camaieu—on Sèvres and other continental china, and even charming little landscape vignettes and landscape backgrounds on Chelsea, Worcester, and Longton Hall pieces; but for pure natural English landscapes on porcelain, the first and most prolific producer was Derby. The greatest and most esteemed of the Old Derby landscape painters was undoubtedly Zachariah Boreman (sometimes spelt Boarman, Boardman, and Bowman in the old Chelsea account books). When Wm. Duesbury of Derby bought and carried on the

Chelsea works we find Boreman continuing to work for him, for his name appears in the old account books kept by the foreman, Richard Barton, as being the head painter at the factory at a wage of 5/3 per day—that was in 1771. On the closing down of the Chelsea Works in 1784 Duesbury induced Boreman to come to Derby, giving him a fixed wage and long term agreement at the increased rate of two guineas a week. At Chelsea Boreman supplemented his 5/3 per day by working overtime. This overtime was done piecework, and seems to have been work of a very humble description—for example, " 30 seals painted in Mottowes (Mottoes) by Boreman & Wollams, 3/1½." " 96 thimbles painted overtime by Boarman & Co., 12/-." "The Mottoes done to 36 seals by Boardman & Wolliams, 3/9 "—it will be seen from the above that the worthy Barton's spelling was (like his Master Duesbury's) not his strong point.

Boreman seems to have worked at Chelsea from some time before 1768 till 1784—then at Derby from 1784 to 1794. After that he returned to London and there he painted for Sims, an old Derby painter who kept an enamelling establishment and enamelled porcelain in the white for the china trade. Boreman died at Pimlico in 1810 aged 72 years.

It is difficult to identify any of Boreman's painting on Chelsea or Chelsea-Derby porcelain. There are certainly no such pieces decorated with the soft, subdued, charmingly painted landscapes which form his well-known work at Derby. Did he only paint the ordinary trade pieces, the services and the figures—the seals and the thimbles? and if so, who then was it painted the fine figure and bird paintings on the beautiful, rich and expensive vases?

Some of these were painted with landscapes in reserves; but we do not recognise Boreman's hand in these—others were painted with figures or birds in reserves—yet Askew who was the figure painter only got 4/2 a day in 1771, and we do not identify his style in the figures painted on these splendid vases. An enlightening indication is given us in one of Barton's accounts, viz.:—" Mr O'Neil, on account, a painter . . . 1. 1. 0 "; one gathers from this that none of the early porcelain factories, Chelsea, Worcester, or Derby (still less the smaller places like

Lowestoft, Longton Hall, Plymouth, Bristol, &c.) employed regularly painters capable of executing the fine figure and other paintings done on their large vases, &c.; but that these latter were always sent to be painted in the reserves by outside artist painters, such as O'Neale, J. Donaldson, and later Thos. Baxter the elder, &c.

The landscapes executed on important pieces of Chelsea, Derby, and the rare Worcester examples, are undoubtedly the work of one hand, and that was the hand of O'Neale. The Fogo myth has probably arisen from a piece signed by Fogg, a later painter, the tail of the last "g" having got erased, probably before firing.

Whatever may have been Boreman's style of painting at Chelsea, however, and Haslem tells us that he was a painter of birds, there is no mistaking the manner and method of his beautiful landscapes and seascapes painted on Derby porcelain, and also painted on porcelain of various descriptions at Sim's establishment in London afterwards.

How then may his work be recognised?

The Landscape Painters

1. Haslem says:—His method was to model, or to use a technical term, to wash in, the subject in neutral tint, over which he laid the positive colours, such as green, red, or yellow, which being transparent allowed the neutral colour to be seen through them. The piece of porcelain thus treated was then fired in the enamelling kiln to fix the painting, and all that was done afterwards before the second and final firing was to hatch and stipple over the foliage and other more detailed parts in a darker or finishing colour with a finer paint-brush, called by china painters a tracing pencil.

Jockey Hill painted in a similar manner. Both painted in a quiet and subdued colouring—the chief points of difference between the two being that whereas Hill hatched and stippled in a light and delicate manner and to a larger extent in the finishing process, Boreman did less stippling and hatching but got his effects with broader washes in the first painting. Boreman's paintings have also less local colour than Hill's, in whose landscapes the greens and yellows are sometimes rather too predominant and out of harmony.

2. The skies are often of an ochre tint with neutral tinted clouds—sometimes the white edges of the clouds and other high lights are wiped off with the pointed wooden end of the paintbrush.

3. Minute but marvellously suggestive figures are often introduced with good effect into the landscape. The tone of the greys and greens, which predominate, have a Corot-like effect very observable in some of his most beautiful examples, and the resemblance is intensified by a vivid touch of red or orange sometimes introduced in the foreground of the picture.

4. As Boreman worked at Derby only between 1784 and 1794 any genuine work done by him would have the following characteristics :—

Only very few, if any, specimens would be marked with the crown and D without batons, as this mark was not used during his time at Derby. Nearly the whole of his work would be marked with the crowned D *with* crossed batons. This is almost always, if not always, in puce or blue—not in red. There is no painter's number with it, as this rule was instituted after he left the Derby Factory—but there would often be a pattern number.

5. The pattern numbers marked in the Old Derby pattern book as being done by Boreman are :—

No. 134. Black upon Moonlight Landskip.
No. 178. Landskip near Critch.
No. 244. Brown Landskip.
No. 260. View from Cheltenham.
No. 264. Coloured Landskip.
No. 330. Landskip.
No. 336. Landskip (in colours).

In addition to these there are No. 50, "View of Dovedale," and other numbers having landscape patterns, often with other views of Dovedale, such as 43, 64, 66, 74, 90, 116, 123, 127, 131, &c.

6. The glaze would be thick and soft, and the

gold enrichment would be of the thick honey gold, not the later burnished brown, or mercury gold.

Two examples are given here, one of Boreman's work at Derby, a beautiful and characteristic "View of Dovedale," and a plate painted by him at Sim's Establishment in London with a most Corot-like view of the river and bridge, Singleton, near Midhurst.

Haslem says he was one of the most celebrated of the Chelsea hands—as a painter of landscapes and birds he was considered unrivalled.

It is very probable therefore that he painted birds on the services at Chelsea, and in this way may have been the painter of the birds on the celebrated Chelsea service presented by Queen Charlotte to her brother the Duke of Mecklenberg and on other services of the same pattern, which were held in high contemporary esteem. The same writer testifies that "his birds, like his landscapes, are softly painted and the colours sober and delicately blended," very different to the bold gorgeous style of the usual bird painting on the later Chelsea china of Sprimont's period.

4. The mark would be a carefully jewelled crown with D and batons, and might be blue, puce, or red.

5. The glaze would be thick and pellucid, the gold of the thick honey quality; but any collector who is fortunate enough to have a specimen of Banford's landscape painting will not only have a very rare and miniature-like piece of work, but surely also a document of very human interest, even if it be the product of "strained optic nerves" at 24/- a week of ten hours.

The last of the Old Derby landscape painters to be mentioned here is Robert Brewer, for this book does not concern itself with the later landscape painters of the nineteenth century. Robert Brewer (as also his brother John, another Old Derby painter) was a native of Madeley, Salop, and had probably been apprenticed at the Caughley or Coalport China Factory, proceeding as a journeyman painter to Worcester; from there he would appear to have come to Derby, joining his elder brother John at the factory. He seems to have been one of the less picturesque but more steady hands—wishful to improve himself he took lessons in painting from the well-known Derby artist, Paul Sandby, and may therefore be described as a fellow pupil of J. M. W. Turner the great landscape artist. He would appear to have commenced work at Derby during the last few years of the eighteenth century and continued there till his brother's death about 1815, when he succeeded to his brother's clientele as a Drawing Master at Derby. Most of the services and vases painted with landscapes at Derby during that period are the work of Robert Brewer, and very good work it is—even if it has not the distinctive qualities of Boreman and Hill. He it was who was chosen to paint the famous service for the then Duke of Devonshire, decorated with views of Chatsworth, Bolton Abbey, &c.

How shall one recognise his work?

1. Well it is not very difficult for he had a distinctive style of his own and that style did not vary greatly in the many pieces decorated by him, and not only did his style remain constant, but his palette of colours also. If

therefore one has a couple of authentic samples to study it is quite easy to identify others. To begin with, his method of painting was quite different to that of the earlier painters, such as Boreman and Hill.

There is no modelling in the neutral tint followed by broad washes of positive colours—on the contrary the landscape is painted straight away in the positive colours; then it received the first firing in the enamel kiln; afterwards it is strengthened and darkened where necessary, receiving heightened detail, and is refired. Chrome greens and warm browns and madders give to the picture a bright and glowing appearance, while the gaiety of the scene is often accentuated by a flag or figures clad in bright primary colours in the foreground. The scenes are well balanced and in excellent perspective, and the worst that can be said of them is that they are sometimes a trifle commonplace and lacking in distinction.

Some characteristics to be noticed are that the sky is generally a pleasant light blue, the blue being painted across the picture from left to right, and cumulous white clouds are swept out, apparently not with the brush but with a rounded stump of paper or wood, leaving rather hard abrupt outlines. These are then shaded with neutral tint and ochre. The trees are painted or shaded in conventional detail with leaves that resemble five points curved upwards, rather like the thumb and fingers of a hand turned upwards and curved, with a space between each digit.

The high lights are often wiped out with the pointed end of the paintbrush handle.

2. Brewer's painting is mostly found on the harder paste and glaze of the later period.

3. The marks are the jewelled crown, crossed batons and D almost always in red, sometimes with pattern number and sometimes without.

4. Being the best landscape painter of his time in the Derby Factory, his work is usually finished with good, often elaborate, gilding: but this is almost always (if indeed it is necessary to qualify the statement at all) in

CHAPTER VI

The Bird and Fruit Painters on Old Derby Porcelain

Bird painting on porcelain was never a speciality of the Old Derby Factory as it was at Chelsea and to some extent at Bow, and at Worcester when the Chelsea bird painters were taken on there about 1758 during the first illness of Sprimont, when for a period the Chelsea Factory was nearly closed down. Later on there was a vogue for dinner and dessert services painted in birds and even some large vases. These were done by Dodson. But in the earlier period such articles as were decorated with birds at Derby were painted by Zachariah Boreman and afterwards by John Brewer.

True Complin, the early fruit painter, painted some pieces with birds, and introduced birds sometimes into his fruit compositions—but these were more in the nature of accessories to the fruit, just as butterflies were often introduced into flower paintings to give an added touch of nature to the composition; for what more natural than that birds should be seen in juxtaposition to fruit or butterflies to flowers.

John Brewer was engaged (we find by his agreement with Wm. Duesbury the second) to paint animals on china, as indeed he was engaged to paint everything else, such as figures, landscapes and flowers, and it may be supposed that as birds are included in the animal kingdom so they were also included in Brewer's duties, for we find in his piecework accounts of 29th April—

2 Coffee Cans and Stands, birds.
1 Dejunée of birds (*sic*).
1 Cream Jug of birds.
1 Teapot of birds.
1 Cream Jug of birds.
1 Teapot of birds.

As there were thirty items in this piecework account, it will be seen that six items out of thirty or twenty per cent. of the whole consisted of bird decoration.

These would be painted between 1795 and 1810.

When John Brewer left Derby the bird

painting was done by Richard Dodson, the son of Wm. Dodson, who succeeded Thos. Soar as foreman over the painters and who died about 1820. Shortly after his death his son Richard Dodson, the bird painter, left the factory and set up for himself as an enameller in Derby.

It may be gathered therefore from the above records that such bird painting on Derby porcelain as was called for was done in each period by one hand, viz.:—

From 1785 to 1795 by Zachariah Boreman.
From 1796 to about 1810 by John Brewer.
From 1810 to about 1821 by Richard Dodson.

To distinguish between their work one must remember

1. The style of the painter. Zachariah Boreman painted exotic birds in the Chelsea manner, thinly painted, beautifully modelled in with grey or neutral tint, washed over with positive colours rather low in tone, *i.e.*, not too bright and glaring—then fired to fix the colours, lastly stippled with the heightened colours where necessary.

2. The green in the landscape or background is the transparent copper green, never the more opaque chrome green.
3. The gilding is always of the soft honey gold variety.
4. The paste or body of the porcelain is the soft earlier body with creamy translucency—the glaze thick and pellucid—very soft and easily scratched.
5. The marks might be very rarely the D and jewelled crown without crossed batons in blue or puce, but nearly always the jewelled crown over crossed batons and D, practically always in blue or puce and rather large—very carefully drawn.

John Brewer's birds also rather favoured the Chelsea manner, but were painted in a different way. The painting is thicker and stands up on the harder glaze in a harder drier manner.

1. The birds, &c., are not drawn in and modelled in neutral tint but are put in straight away in their natural colours, receiving then their first firing, and are afterwards hatched over and heightened with brighter and deeper colours and refired,

They are very neatly and carefully finished.

The backgrounds or branches are painted in chrome green with other colours and the gold is burnished.

2. The paste is of the harder kind that came in at Duesbury's (II) death in 1796, with a greenish translucency and a thinner uncrazed glaze to correspond.
3. Marks would be invariably the jewelled crown, crossed batons and D in red; often with a pattern number, and sometimes with a gilder's number; though the rare D K mark is not ruled out.

Richard Dodson painted his birds in extremely bright and gay colours. They cannot be described exactly as exotic birds, but rather as natural birds in unnaturally gay plumage. Thus even a peacock with outspread tail is painted with far more colour than its original, while other birds are almost unrecognisable in their fancy costumes.

There are generally a good many birds on one piece, and these are usually disposed in naturalistic landscapes and are engaged in doing what they might naturally be occupied in. Thus peacocks are strutting about, kingfishers are fishing in a stream and quite possibly have proved successful in annexing a small fish, and so on.

These services, or other pieces, are exceedingly bright and gay, but are rather garish and unnatural and offend a refined taste.

In this they differ from the bright coloured exotic birds of the Chelsea, Bow, Longton Hall, and Worcester early periods. These may be said to be like nothing on earth; but neither do they pretend to be. There is something fantastic yet harmonious about the latter which makes them to be in perfect taste, with a sort of faëry-like naturalness of their own. Fantaisie Vögel as the old-world Saxons used to call them—Birds of Phantasy. They come bright-eyed and glowing straight from the realms of imagination like the fairy tales of Grimm and of Hans Andersen.

Richard Dodson's bird painting was all done between about 1810 and 1821—therefore

1. It would be painted on the softer porcelain, often with a green translucency, which came in again in about 1810, with a thick, soft glaze nearly always crazed. This crazing is caused

by the glaze and body not contracting equally, *i.e.*, the glaze is chemically incorrect for use with that particular body. It is often, too, the result of insufficient firing of the body.

2. All would be done during first Michael Kean's and then Robert Bloor's proprietorship and management of the Derby Factory, and would therefore be marked with the crown, crossed batons, and D in red, carelessly drawn, rather small, and the crown jewelled or unjewelled, or with the usual thumb-printed marks of the Bloor period.
3. The gold would always be of the modern burnished mercury gold kind, often with borders of " Empire " style in gold.
4. The mark would generally be accompanied by a number.
5. Dodson's name only appears once in the Old Derby pattern books, viz.:—

No. 575. Red Arrabesk by Dodson and Torkington.

As Torkington was an Arabesque painter and

gilder, this probably means that the pieces in question were painted with birds by Dodson and with red Arabesque border by Torkington; just as we find later No. 599 painted by Stansby (presumably with flowers, as he was a flower painter) gilt by Torkington.

The two fruit painters at Derby were:—

During the early period, Geo. Complin.
During the later period, Thos. Steele.

George Complin must have been one of the earliest painters at the Old Derby Factory. He would appear to have been a Frenchman, probably brought to Chelsea by Sprimont about 1755 and finding work at Derby about 1758, when the Chelsea Factory was practically closed down for a time owing to Sprimont's illness.

He seems to have worked at Derby till about 1795, when he may either have returned to France or died. His fruit painting when once seen is unmistakeable, though it is not often seen, in spite of the fact that Complin worked for many years at Derby and must have turned out a good deal of work. His fruit is painted in a conventional, not a naturalistic, manner and is exceedingly bright and gay, a sort of riot of colour; but pleasing in effect and very decorative. Complin's style reminds one of that of the unnamed Meissen artist at Chelsea, who painted fruit, birds, and butterflies in such a gay and distinctive manner, and who afterwards decorated Worcester porcelain in the same style; but the one would never be mistaken for the other. Complin's birds on the other hand are not of the exotic variety but are natural birds, such as tomtits, chaffinches, bullfinches, &c. (usually small birds), conventionally painted in gay, bright colours.

Haslem says:—"Sometimes he introduced small animals and birds among the fruit, and he did not always preserve the proper or relative proportions, a squirrel for instance not being much larger than a mouse, judging by the size of the fruit by which he is surrounded." And he goes on to mention examples in which this peculiarity occurs. He adds—"these pieces . . . are rich in colour."

1. A good many pieces decorated by Complin are unmarked; but when marked they would

have the jewelled crown and D with and without batons and almost always in blue or puce—always of course overglaze.

2. The paste would be the early body, soft and with a creamy translucency. The glaze would be thick and pellucid. The gilding of the soft honey gold and usually rather sparse.

3. The patterns marked in the Old Derby pattern books to be done by Complin are :—

No. 136. Fruit by Complin. Upon Landskip Background.
No. 138. Fruit by Complin.
No. 140. Fruit by Complin.
No. 150. Birds and Landskip by Complin.
No. 236. Fruit and Birds by Complin.
No. 237. Fruit and Birds by Complin.
No. 245. Fruit by Complin, with Tomtit and Bullfinch before Dark Landskip.
No. 254. Fruit and Birds by Complin.
No. 259. Fruit and Birds by Complin.
No. 261. Fruit and Birds by Complin.
No. 325. Fruit and Flowers by Complin.

There appears therefore to have been a specially large demand for Complin's painting, his name being specified no less than eleven times in the Old Derby pattern book as against fourteen times for Banford (the most in demand of all), seven for Boreman, nine for Billingsley, five for Askew, and twelve divided between the two Brewer brothers.

There are two or three personal touches in the porcelain records which give us just a glimpse of the character and personality of this charming old-time painter :—

We gather from Bernice Banford's letter, and from the absence of his signature from the men painters' petition to Wm. Duesbury asking him not to give out work to women painters that he had a soft heart for the opposite sex, and was not afraid to stand out against all the rest for what he thought just and right.

In a letter dated 18th September, 1794, he says :—" I think my hair (his grey or white hair due to advanced age) admits of more respect " ——and speaks of his employment " the variety I do, and the variableness of the work."

He probably left the factory with so many

others of the old hands when Kean began to manage it in 1795, and their old master Wm. Duesbury the second lay dying. Old hands do not like a new master, and possibly the loss at one time of such masters of their art as Billingsley, Banford, Boreman, Askew, and Complin was the beginning of the decline of this charming old factory, which continued to its close in Robert Bloor's time, or soon after.

However, for the moment all were replaced with some vigour. Pegg the Quaker takes the place of Billingsley in flower painting; John Brewer succeeds Banford in painting figures, and Complin in delineating fruit and birds—Robert Brewer follows Boreman and does the landscape painting, and so on.

Distinction has gone; but well painted, artistic decoration is still in evidence.

When John Brewer too had left, and once more in course of time fruit painting was in demand, Thomas Steele the elder was engaged, that was in 1815. It is possible that Robert Brewer did any fruit painting (and there was not much) required till then.

Haslem speaks with unbounded admiration of

CHAPTER VII

A Chronology of Old Derby Porcelain

In deciding the origin, date, and individuality of any pieces of old porcelain, it is necessary to know something of the paste, glaze, translucency,[7] colours, gilding, and decoration of each factory; and also the changes, and especially the dates of the changes, in all these particulars which took place periodically at each factory.

The diagnosis of a piece of porcelain is very similar to the diagnosis of a human ailment, which is perhaps one reason why Collectors of old china number so many Doctors in their ranks.

The Author once knew a Doctor who had passed all his examinations brilliantly, who had all the phases of disease, all the symptoms, and all the remedies at his finger ends; but yet failed in the one thing necessary—the gift of diagnosis. It is much the same with a Collector of old porcelain. He may have all the knowledge available, an intense interest in his subject, great application to his hobby; but if he is unable to decide with certainty which is hard[8] and which is soft paste porcelain, which paste or glaze was made at Derby, which at Chelsea, Worcester, Bow, &c., no book ever written will endow him with this gift.

The greatest help to this knowledge, however, is an accurate and exhaustive chronology, by which a piece may be tested point by point.

An accurate result may in this way be easily arrived at by the familiar process of elimination. The most perfect chronology of Old Derby porcelain ever yet compiled is presented below:

CHRONOLOGY OF OLD DERBY PORCELAIN.

1724—Wm. Littler of Longton Hall born.
1725 Wm. Duesbury I. born.
1727 George II. began to reign—died 1760.
1727 Andrew Planché born.
1742 Wm. Duesbury I. started enamelling work in London; aged 17 years.
1745 Andrew Planché making small porcelain figures in Derby; aged 18 years.

A Chronology

1746 to 1750 Date of manufacture of small moulded porcelain Cream Jugs in British Museum and Victoria and Albert Museum marked with large incised script D (latter 1750).

1746 Messrs. Butts, Rivett & Heath, under style of the Derby Porcelain Manufactory commenced making porcelain at the Cockpit Hill Pot Works with Planché as arcanist.

1751—1753 Wm. Duesbury I. carrying on an enamelling business in London on his own account, decorating Bow, Chelsea, Derby (Cockpit Hill) and Staffordshire (Longton Hall) figures, &c., as per his account books.

1754 Wm. Duesbury left London and resided at Longton Hall with his father, also named Wm. Duesbury, but kept on business of enamelling in London.

1755 Wm. Duesbury Ist's father (a currier of Cannock) made over to him his small property, on condition that his son kept him in comfort during the remainder of his lifetime—a condition faithfully carried out. His father died in 1768.

1755 Wm. Duesbury I. returned to London finding Littler quite impracticable.

1755 Wm. Duesbury's father makes over his property to Wm. Duesbury I. to enable him to open the factory on the Nottingham Road. Manufacture of porcelain ceases at Cockpit Hill Factory.

1756 Draft agreement dated 1st January between John Heath, Andrew Planché, and Wm. Duesbury drawn out, but never signed.

1755—1756 Property on Nottingham Road acquired and adapted for new porcelain factory.

1756 Wm. Duesbury I. starts business there by himself; but supported with loan from Heath. Planché in difficulties owing to immoral life, drops out.

1756 Nottingham Road Factory carried on by Wm. Duesbury I.

1756 Auction Sale in December in London 'by order of the proprietors of the Derby Porcelain Factory'—*N.B.* Butt, Rivett and Heath, getting rid of their stock after closing the manufacture of porcelain at the Cockpit Hill Factory.

1757 Paragraph appeared in the "Public Advertiser" saying good judges could not tell Derby figures from those made at Dresden. *N.B.*—This would refer to Wm. Duesbury Ist's manufacture.)

1758 Longton Hall Works closed. Derby (Nottingham Road) Factory enlarged and number of hands engaged doubled.

1758 Partnership between Wm. Littler of Longton Hall and Wm. Duesbury I. begun 1754 brought to an end.

1760 George III. began to reign—died in 1820. Regency 1788-1820.

1763 Forty-two boxes of porcelain goods sent to London for sale; realised £666 17s. 6d.

1764 Richard Holdship came to Derby from the Worcester Factory. Derby printed ware and steatitic body commenced same date.

1769 August 17th. Duesbury I. arranged for purchase of Chelsea Factory. F. Duvivier began painting flowers at Derby.

1770—1784—Chelsea-Derby mark  at Chelsea under Duesbury's proprietorship.

1770 February 5th. Purchase of Chelsea works completed—Church says biscuit figures first made at this date.

1770 Action against Francis Thomas and Burnsall *re* Chelsea stock.

1770 P. Stephan, modeller, commenced work at Derby—supplied models till 1795.

1770 Special quality biscuit figures made from this date till 1810. Afterwards secret lost, and ordinary unglazed body made.

1770 Edward Withers comes to Derby.

1771 Nicolas Sprimont of Chelsea died. Derby biscuit figures first mentioned in sale catalogues. (First " Chelsea and Derby " Catalogue.)

1772 R. Askew, figure subject painter, came from Chelsea to Derby.

1772 Jonathan Wedgwood employed as thrower and repairer.

1773  mark (in gold) used at Chelsea till 1784  mark at Derby till 1782.

1773 London Warehouse opened in Old Castle Tavern, Bedford Street. George III. gave his Royal patronage—Crown added to mark.

1773 Wm. Wood installed as London Agent, and issued lists of articles for sale (later succeeded by Lygo). Among these biscuit groups of the King (George III.), Queen, and Royal Family.

Figures of Muses and of Virtues mentioned in catalogue (Second "Chelsea and Derby" Catalogue.)

1774 Wm. Billingsley apprenticed—16 years old (born 1758). Left Derby 1796.

1775

1776 Wm. Duesbury I. bought and closed Bow Porcelain Factory and moved some moulds and workmen to Derby.

1777

1778 Sale of Derby porcelain; sale of remainder of Chelsea porcelain.

1779 Sale of remainder of Chelsea porcelain.

1780 Catalogue of sale of ' Derby and Chelsea ' porcelain. Heath became bankrupt. Derby and Chelsea properties transferred by deed to Duesbury alone—on paying off mortgage or loan from Heath, secured on these properties.

1781 Catalogue of sale of ' Derby and Chelsea ' porcelain.

1782 Catalogue of sale of ' Derby and Chelsea ' porcelain.

mark commenced—almost always in blue and puce till 1795, in red afterwards—ceased 1830.

1783 Catalogue of sale of ' Derby and Chelsea ' porcelain.

1782—Smith's ground colour blue, called Lapis Lazuli blue, discontinued and the " Ultramarine Blue," or underglaze blue, substituted.

1784 Sale of ' Derby and Chelsea ' porcelain. Chelsea Works closed down and models and workmen taken to Derby, viz.:— Boreman, Boyer, &c. Zachariah Boreman starts at Derby.

1785 Duesbury's annual catalogue of his Derby porcelain published. Sam. Keys apprenticed.

1786 Wm. Duesbury II. taken into partnership—Firm styled "Wm. Duesbury & Son."

1786 Towards the end of the year (Novr.) Wm. Duesbury I. died. Wm. Duesbury II. becomes sole proprietor.

1787 Firm styled once more "Wm. Duesbury." Wm. Duesbury III. born.

1788 Prince Regent appointed owing to George III.'s insanity.

1789 Batt printing introduced by Wm. Duesbury II.

1789 Cream ware (earthenware resembling Wedgwood's Queen's ware) was made for a short time at the Derby Factory.

1790 Jas. Banford began work at Derby—left 1795. J. J. Spängler began work at Derby; but had supplied Duesbury with models from London before that date.

1791 W. J. Coffee came to Derby.

1792

1793

1794 Zachariah Boreman leaves Derby Factory.

1795 Wm. Duesbury II. in failing health—takes Michael Kean into partnership. Banford and Billingsley leave the factory. Quaker Pegg starts work at Derby.

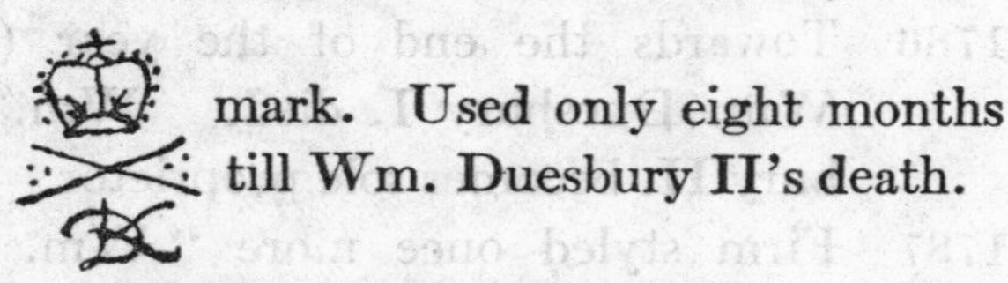
mark. Used only eight months till Wm. Duesbury II's death.

1795 John Brewer is engaged; also George Robertson.

1796 Wm. Duesbury II. died. Michael Kean carries on the Factory for the family. Mark now is 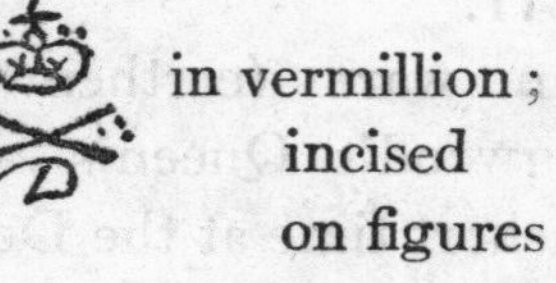 in vermillion; incised on figures 

1808 Wm. Duesbury III., aged 21, marries Annabella Sheffield, daughter of Wm. E.

Sheffield of the Polygon, Somers Town, London.

1811 Kean retired. Wm. E. Sheffield bought his share and the style of the firm became "Duesbury & Sheffield." Mark remained as above.

1815 Duesbury III. leased business to Robert Bloor. End of Napoleonic wars. Mark became  always in red, *i.e.*, crown carelessly drawn and smaller, not jewelled. Often pattern number below. Used till 1830.

1820 George IV. ascended the throne. Bloor appointed manufacturer to Royalty. "Bloor Derby" round crown, and elaborate crown over  printed "thumb"—marks in red used till 1845.

1828 Robt. Bloor became insane. Factory carried on by his Manager, Thomason, for family.

1845 Robt. Bloor died. Works carried on and gradually closed down by Thos. Clarke.

1848 Factory finally closed down and models sold to Saml. Boyle of Fenton.

MARKS ON OLD DERBY PORCELAIN.

1745—1750  (Incised) on two known specimens.

1765—1780 N Sometimes incised, sometimes in red or blue, sometimes alone, at others with  mark.

1770—1782  Usually in puce or blue, more rarely in gold and other colours—never underglaze.

1782—1795 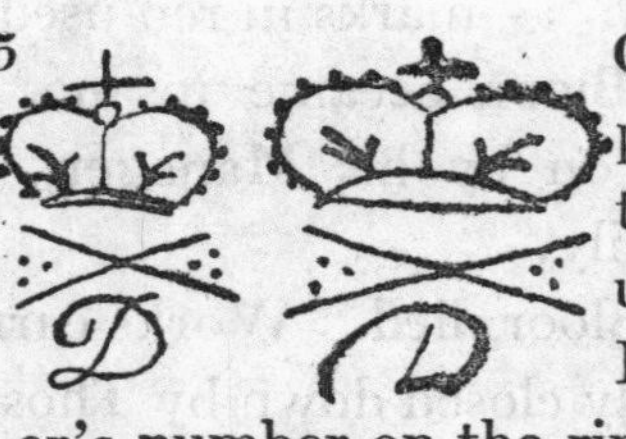 Often accompanied by pattern number underneath the D, and by gilder's number on the rim. Incised on figures. Usually in puce or blue.

1795—1796 **Usually in red.**

1796—1814

In red and incised on figures. Figures usually bore other signs, No. 195—(*a*) The pattern number, *e.g.*, No. 195; (*b*) the size, *e.g.*, 5 *size*; (*c*) the repairer's sign, *e.g.*, for Jos. Hill, for Isaac Farnsworth.

1715—1820

Almost always in red, rarely in gold.

Old Derby Porcelain

1820—1848

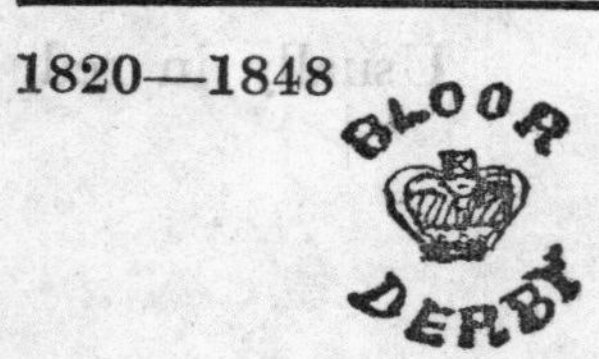

On best quality porcelain, always printed and in vermillion.

Besides these—Oriental, Continental, and other marks were more or less accurately copied.

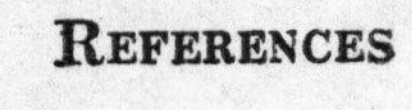

References

References

Ref. No. 1.—New Avenues of Knowledge.

This refers particularly to fresh light on the artistic side of the early Derby porcelain, on the bodies, glazes, and colours, gilding, &c., at various periods; and to the identification of the work of the various artist-workmen. Also it refers to the illustrations; many of which are unique, and most hitherto unpublished.

The writer does not claim to produce here new historical facts; he does, however, attempt, it is hoped not unsuccessfully, to bring the varying and contradictory statements of former writers into a historically correct and coherent sequence.

This may be proved by comparing the fairly exhaustive references annexed:—

Andrew Planche.

Jewitt's *Ceramic Art in Great Britain*, 1st Ed., Vol. I, pages 57, 63, 64, 65, 66, 67; 2nd Ed., 1883, pp. 334, 335.

Chaffer's *Marks and Monograms*, 11th Ed., 1906, page 793.

Haslem's *Old Derby China Factory*, pages 17, 18.

Bemrose's *Bow Chelsea and Derby Porcelain*, pages 18, 19, 103-106; *Longton Hall Porcelain*, page 6.

Solon's *Old English Porcelain*, pages 85, 86.

Moore Binn's *First Century of English Porcelain*, pages 124, 125.

Nightingale's *Contributions Towards the History of Early English Porcelain*, pages lvi, lix, lxvii.

REF. NO. 2.—JOHN HEATH.

Jewitt's *Ceramic Art in Great Britain*, 1878, Vol. II, pages 57-69, 89.

Chaffer's *Marks and Monograms*, 11th Ed., 1906, pages 791-793.

Haslem's *Old Derby China Factory*, pages 17, 18.

References

Bemrose's *Bow, Chelsea and Derby Porcelain*, pages 101-103, 106, 109; *Longton Hall Porcelain*, page 6.

Solon's *Old English Porcelain*, page 85.

Ref. No. 3.

Some writers throw doubt on the fact that Andrew Planché could have been modelling small figures and carrying on a tiny manufactory on his own account at the age of 17 years and upward. But nobody who is acquainted with the working life of the Potteries districts in those days, or even fifty years ago, before the great modern developments of Combines and Trades Unions, will feel any surprise at such a fact. William Duesbury himself is a contemporary example of the same business precocity; for he could have been very little older than this when he set up his little decorating establishment in London. The same style of criticism would make it impossible for a young man of twenty-six to be Prime Minister of England, had not Pitt the younger proved its possibility historically.

Ref. No. 4.

Heath.

Jewitt's *Ceramic Art in Great Britain*, 1st Ed., 1878, Vol. I, pp. 215, 232; Vol. II, pp. 57-69, 89.

It may be objected by some that if Jewitt's and Bemrose's conclusion that the partnership between Duesbury, Heath, and Planché was never consummated were correct, how came Heath's name to be associated with that of Duesbury in the agreements made respectively with Richard Holdship with regard to the supply of Soapstone (Steatite) in 1764 and with James Cox for the leasing of the Chelsea Porcelain Factory in 1769.

Any owner of a factory, any banker, or any lawyer with experience of such matters, however, would be able to show the unreliability of this objection. For granted that Heath the Banker lent Duesbury the Factory Proprietor a certain amount of capital to start and work his business, which is established, that banker would require security for his money while so lent. This security would take the form of a mortgage or first charge on the factory, stock, and business generally, and all the deeds would be deposited with the banker.

Until the sum advanced was repaid, with all interest accruing, no legal agreement, lease, purchase, or sale of property could be entered into without the consent of the lender on mortgage. Even presuming that by the time of the lease of the Chelsea factory, Duesbury had been able to pay off the original loan or advance (an unlikely supposition in the case of a man, like Duesbury, who was always extending and enlarging his business), the same conditions would arise should Duesbury require a fresh or further advance for the purchase of the Chelsea business and lease of premises; almost a certainty in the case of a man, like Duesbury, of no large personal capital and of go-ahead methods. That Heath was still acting as Duesbury's banker is proved by the accounts of James Giles's debts to Duesbury quoted by Jewitt (*Ceramic Art in Great Britain*, 1878 Ed., Vol. I, p. 215):—

"Paid Mr. Heath a Bill on Mr. Giles dated Feb. 20, at 2 months value £120."

If Heath were a partner Duesbury would not pay him Giles's bill at 2 months; but Duesbury would certainly pay it in to Heath as his banker.

It is true that in the lease of the Chelsea Factory premises, &c., quoted by Bemrose (*Bow, Chelsea, and Derby Porcelain*, p. 28), both Duesbury and Heath are described as "Porcelaine Manufacturers"; this can easily be explained by the fact that Heath actually was a porcelain manufacturer in virtue of his partnership in the Cockpit Hill business, and by the quite natural supposition that Duesbury would rather account for the presence of his name in the Deeds in this way than as the holder of a mortgage on his factory.

On the other hand there is no known instance of Heath's name being associated with that of Duesbury on any other than a legal document. Thus in the invoice of 7th November, 1771, for goods supplied to Philip Egerton, Esq., quoted by Chaffers (*Marks & Monograms*, 1906, p. 805), is printed "Bot of William Duesbury & Co., Derby." Not Duesbury & Heath; also in that of August, 1777. In the various apprenticeship indentures, *e.g.*, Wm. Billingsley's, there is no mention of Heath. In the mark, there is no monogram of D. & H.; though when Kean is brought into partnership there is a D K monogram.

The whole weight of evidence available therefore is against the theory that John Heath was ever a partner in the Nottingham Road business, or anything more than a banker who had lent money to start, and possibly to enlarge and extend the business, on the security of business, buildings, stock, and property, leases, &c.

Again, it may be argued that as the firm is frequently styled "Duesbury & Co." on invoices and in advertisements, that the "Co." included Heath. But quite apart from the fact that a great many one-man companies style themselves A. B. & Co., &c., a quite common proceeding then and now, it must be remembered that Heath was an important personage: a banker, a gentleman of birth, a man of some wealth and position (he was twice Mayor of Derby), while Duesbury was a small man, of small means, and the son of a small working currier of Cannock. Consequently if Heath had been in the firm, his name would certainly have come first, just as it actually did in the agreement under review, and the name of the firm would either have been "Heath, Planché & Duesbury," or "Heath & Co."

Ref. No. 5.

CHROME GREEN.

This metallic colour is made from oxide of chromium. It is an opaque colour with a yellowish shade and has more body than copper green.

Having only been discovered about 1795 its presence on a piece indicates that that piece was not made, or at any rate decorated, till after that date.

Ref. No. 6.

COPPER GREEN.

The copper green is so called because it is made from oxide of copper fritted with a flux and ground to a powder. In its pure state it has a bright transparent appearance, and when washed over a design painted in brown, neutral tint or black, allows the design to be seen through. It is a bright green, but can be made into a yellow green by harder firing, or by adding oxide of uranium.

The opaque apple green ground of Worcester is a copper green, but obtains a certain opacity by admixture with a stanniferous base (oxide of tin).

It is of great antiquity, having been used for many hundred years by the Chinese in their "Famille Verte" porcelain.

Ref. No. 7.

TRANSLUCENCY.

One of the most helpful ways of determining the origin, approximate date, and method of manufacture of a specimen of porcelain, is to examine it by transmitted light.

The best way to do this is to hold up the piece of china against an electric light bulb or in front of any strong light, being careful to have no other light in the room shining in front of the object, and place between the light and the article to be examined a piece of matt black cardboard, or other non-reflecting material, with a hole in it, the cardboard being considerably larger than the article to be examined, and the hole considerably smaller than the object.

Hold the plate or other piece, with the decoration away from one.

For a hollow piece, or figure, a good plan is to hold a small electric bulb inside the piece, covering the orifice, and conducting operations in a dark or semi-dark room.

In this way it is possible to examine the translucency of the piece of porcelain, and to see something of its texture.

For instance the colour may be seen, whether a creamy shade as in earliest Bow, Chelsea, and Derby—or a yellowish green translucency as in Dr. Wall Worcester or early Lowestoft, or an orange shade as in Caughley. The light will show up the pin points of light in early triangle marked Chelsea, the moonlike discs in red anchor and seal anchor marked Chelsea.

Coming to Derby porcelain it will make it easy for one to decide of two unmarked pieces decorated and moulded exactly alike, each with a border, say, of Smith's distinctive lapis-lazuli blue, and Derby-styled flowers, which was made at Wm. Duesbury's Derby Works and which at his Chelsea Factory—possibly in the same year. For the translucency of the Chelsea piece will show a multitude of small starlike points of light in the body, while the Derby specimen will show none; phosphatic Derby paste (*i.e.*, having calcined bones in the body) will have a greater translucency, and often in Derby paste a bluish-green tint, due to cupreous impurities in the body—ergo the piece was made after 1770, when bones were introduced from Chelsea.

The presence of steatite or soapstone reduces translucency, gives a dirty yellow tint, and an appearance like looking through thin parchment; almost mottled, or unequal, in its semi-opacity. The piece of Derby porcelain showing this type of translucency will not be earlier than 1764, the date at which Holdship introduced steatite into Derby.

Sometimes a greenish translucency is introduced by the use of smalts (or zaffre), a ground glass frit containing oxide of Cobalt, in the glaze, or even in the body, to correct the yellowish tint of either, just as "Reckitt's blue" is used in washing, to correct the yellowish tint of linen.

Its presence in the glaze is easy to detect from the bluish tint of the glaze ; but in the body it is difficult, if not impossible, to say whether the bluish-green tint is due to the presence of Cobalt or cupreous impurities.

Ref. No. 8.

PORCELAIN is roughly divided into two classes, usually named

1. Hard paste, or natural porcelain, composed of china clay (kaolin) and china stone (petuntse). The china clay is a white infusible earth, the china stone is a white fusible, and therefore vitrifiable, stone—both, when freed from metallic oxides or other impurities, are pure white, and remain pure white when fired.

   The china stone is the binding and fluxing material, and its fusibility is increased by the addition of small proportions of alkalies, such as potash, soda, &c., or lime.

   The proportions in which these materials are employed is legion.

2. Soft paste or artificial porcelain (more correctly named "frit porcelain"). This is composed of some more or less infusible white earth, such as china clay, steatite (soapstone, talc, &c.), and/or calcined bones, for its china clay substitute, and glass in some form, usually called a frit, because its constituents were fritted together in a crucible, or other vessel, till it became a glass. This glass was ground up in water and added to the china clay substitute, thus giving it coherence and translucency. Naturally this artificial china (and its glaze) is softer, both to the file and in its fracture and appearance, than the hard paste or natural porcelain. The softer the paste too, the thicker and softer the glaze, which thus absorbs the metallic oxides painted on it, and is thus responsible for the much greater beauty and artistic feeling of porcelain pieces made of soft paste and glazed with a soft glaze.

Again a soft glaze in its turn takes a thicker, softer, richer-toned gilding. On a very hard glaze gold will only adhere with difficulty and in thin substance.

Old Derby Porcelain

All the old English factories had many changes in their pastes and glazes. Indeed they were always experimenting and changing. But at Derby the paste and glaze changed oftener than at any other. At first the body was like that of early Chelsea creamy with thickish glaze.

When Richard Holdship came to Duesbury from Worcester with his offer of soapstone in 1764 the Derby paste became steatitic.

Again when Duesbury absorbed the Chelsea Factory in 1770 he had bone ash sent from there to Derby, and the paste became phosphatic; but both pastes were made also simultaneously. And above all, collectors and museum authorities, who know nothing of the working of a china factory, always ignore the fact that in slack times immense quantities of ware, especially services of all kinds and useful china, but also figures and vases (for all hands must be kept employed—a factory cannot afford to lose its good and trained workpeople), are made in the white, some in biscuit only—some glazed—and are stocked in the warehouses till busier times, when they are glazed (if in biscuit) and decorated either for sale or to order.

Thus a given piece of porcelain may be made one, five, ten, twenty, and even more years before it is finally decorated and sold.

The style and material of the paste and/or glaze may be years anterior to the style and material of its decoration.

However, except for a comparatively short period, these are rather the exception than the rule; or the unfortunate collector would have even more difficulty in identifying his specimens than he has already.

Derby porcelain, except in the later period following the close of the Napoleonic wars, *i.e.*, from 1815 to 1825, is less liable to this long period of stocking in the white, than many other factories. Chelsea, for instance, during Sprimont's long illness, Bow during Weatherby's bankruptcy, Sèvres after its discovery of hard-paste porcelain, and the consequent supression of its beautiful pâte tendre (the bugbear of collectors—for thousands of pieces were sold in the white glazed state, and, " Decorés dehors," *i.e.*, decorated outside the Royal Factory), Swansea, when Dillwyn leased the factory to Bevington, and others.

Ref. No. 9.

" SOFT PASTE."

A more scientifically accurate and satisfactory name for " soft paste " or artificial porcelain (and one which the Author would like to see universally adopted) is " frit paste " or " frit body." For this term really covers the true difference between all the old artificial porcelains and the hard paste or natural porcelains, inasmuch as a proportion of frit (*i.e.*, fused and levigated glass) enters into the composition of all the old artificial porcelains without exception, English and Continental. Whereas no natural or true porcelain (the hard paste porcelain so called) has any kind of frit in its composition.

On the other hand some soft paste porcelains (Worcester and Bow at certain periods for example) are hard to the file, and some hard paste porcelains (Oriental and Plymouth of certain periods for instance) are soft to the file.

All other designations than this (" frit porcelain ") for artificial porcelain, are difficult to justify under all conditions, and are liable to mislead the uninitiated.

Hard porcelain might be called "true porcelain."

The beautiful hybrid porcelain first invented by Spode and now in use all over England, consisting of the ingredients of "true porcelain" with the addition of calcined bones, might well retain its present trade name of "bone porcelain."

Ref. No. 10.

ARTIST-WORKMEN.

This work does not profess to give a list of all the modellers and painters who worked at Derby Porcelain Factory, any more than it professes to give a complete detailed history of the Factory and its productions. It is intended only to give an account of those whom the Author ventures to call the artist-workmen, as opposed to the mere painting hands; and of those, mainly only those of the eighteenth century, the later developments being, except in rare instances, of less interest to the collector. Any who desire a complete list of the various workmen will be able to compile a fairly comprehensive one from the works of Haslem, Moore Binns, Jewitt, and Bemrose.

For the same reason the accounts given of the various artist-workmen are not always given in chronological order; but rather in the order of their individual interest, artistic or personal.

For a similar reason too, the source of his historical facts having been acknowledged, the Author has omitted always to enclose quotations in inverted commas. Too free a use of these tends to distract the reader and interrupt the easy flow of the narrative.

PLATE 1

PLATE 2

A Rare Handleless Teacup of Derby Porcelain, *circa* 1775, painted in underglaze blue (Smith's Blue being used with indifferent results) and marked with a Crowned *D* in blue underglaze.

(In the Author's Collection.)

PLATE 2

PLATE 3

Figure-Group of a Pair of Lambs lying in a natural attitude. In white glazed old Derby Porcelain, modelled by Andrew Planché at the age of 17 years, and marked with an incised quinquangle ⬠ *circa* 1745.

(In the Author's Collection.)

PLATE 3

PLATE 4

Early Derby Porcelain Sauceboat. Marked with a script N in red. With red floral border in the Kakiemon manner, and Derby flowers.

(In the Author's Collection.)

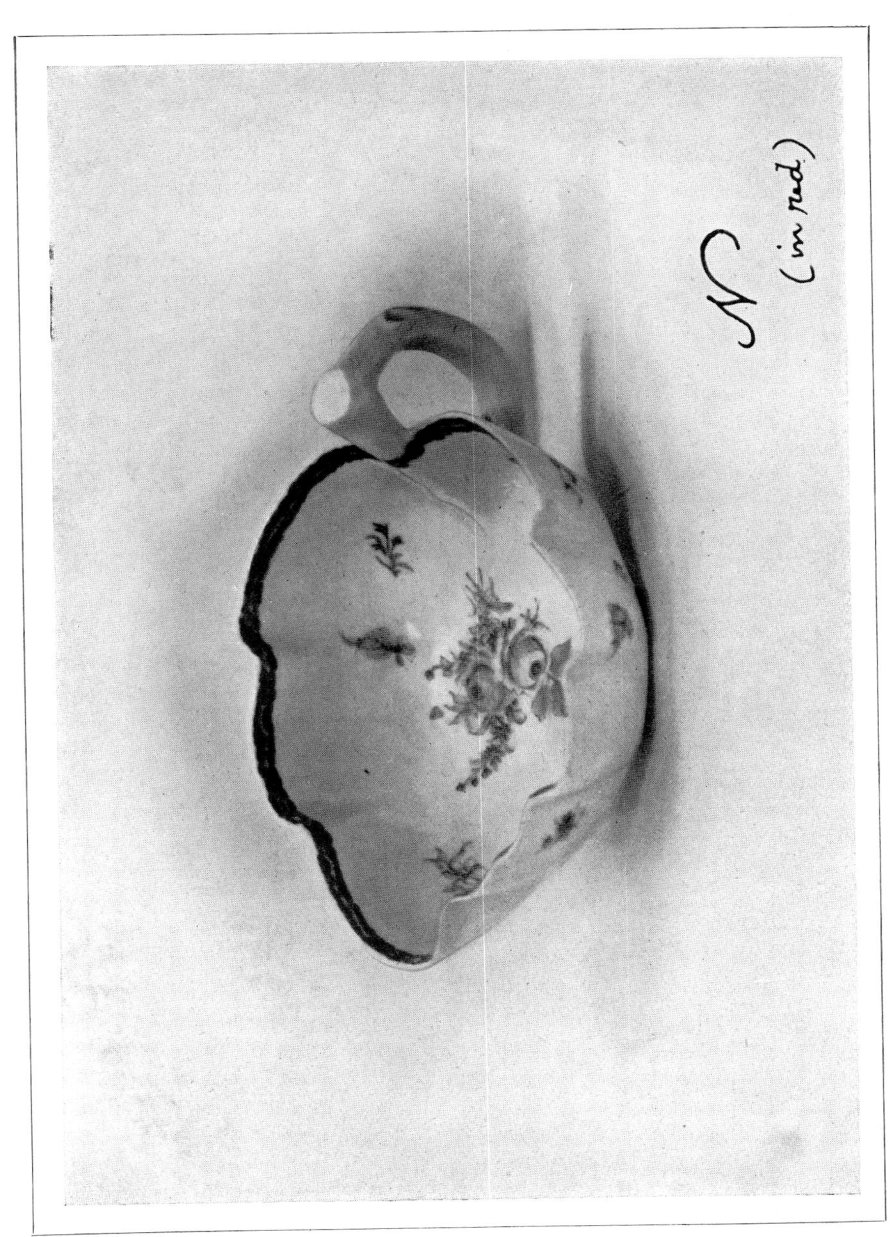

PLATE 4

PLATE 5

Large Sized Britannia (figure in Old Derby Porcelain). Listed in Duesbury's consignment of porcelain pieces sent to London for sale in 1763. Height 14".

(In the Author's Collection.)

PLATE 5

PLATE 6

(Chapter I.)

A Pair of Old Derby ' Candle Vases.' So called because by inverting the covers, the vases become candlesticks. Height 6½″.

When the candles have been burning for an evening, and are half burnt down, the covers can be replaced in position without disturbing the candles, which then hang top downwards inside the vases, ready to be turned up again next evening. A quaint and ingenious arrangement. These candle vases are lot No. 52 in William Duesbury's London Sale Catalogue of 1774-1775. (See Bemrose's " Bow Chelsea and Derby Porcelain," page 59.) Mark No. 4 in red.

(In the Author's Collection.)

PLATE 6

PLATE 7

(Chapter I.)

Large Group of 'Leda' in Old Derby Porcelain, mentioned in the list of Duesbury's consignment of china sent to London for sale in 1763. Height 12″, or with pedestal, $15\frac{1}{4}$″.

(In the Author's Collection.)

PLATE 7

PLATE 8

(Chapter I.)

Jardinière of Barr Flight & Barr's Worcester Porcelain, painted by William Billingsley at Worcester in 1809-1810. Compare with Derby Ewer and Basin painted fifteen or sixteen years earlier. Height, 9½″; width, 9″.

(In the Author's Collection.)

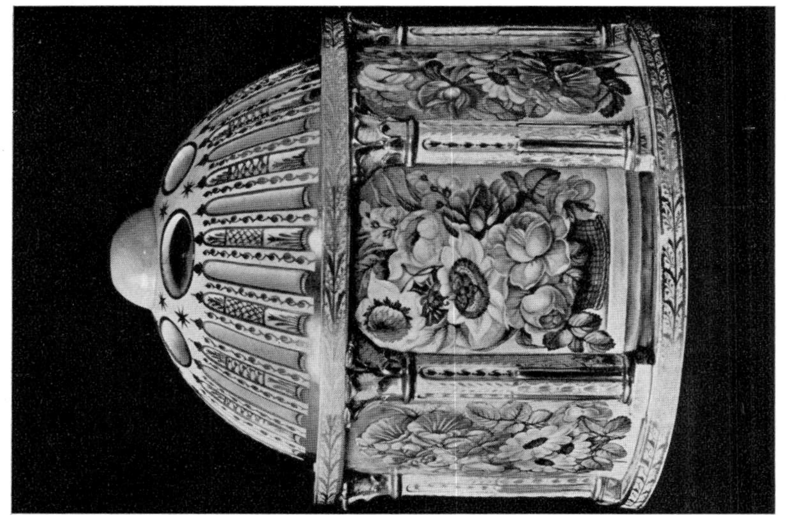

PLATE 8

PLATE 9

(Chapter [illegible])

Large Jug 9" high in Old Derby Porcelain decorated with borders of Smith's [illegible] and gilt, and painted with flowers by Edward Withers. Marked Crown over [illegible]

(In the Author's Collection)

PLATE 9

(Chapter I.)

Large Jug 9″ high in Old Derby Porcelain, decorated with borders of Smith's Lapis Lazuli Blue and rich gilding, and painted with flowers, by Edward Withers. Marked Crown over *D* in blue.

(In the Author's Collection.)

PLATE 9

PLATE 10

(Chapter I.)

Pair of Old Derby Porcelain "Toilet" Figure Candlesticks, mentioned in Duesbury's London Catalogues. So called because they had handles at the back to carry them upstairs by. Very quaint. Height $9\frac{1}{4}''$

(In the Author's Collection.)

PLATE 10

PLATE 11

(Chapter II.)

Three of the Finest Biscuit Groups produced at Derby, viz.: — No. 195. — "Two Virgins Awakening Cupid," modelled by J. J. Spangler, moulded by Isaac Farnsworth. Marked with his mark ✳ a Six Pointed Star. Also No. 195 (Height 12″.

No. 235.—" Three Maidens Distressing Cupid," Modelled by J. J. Spangler. (Height 14½″.) Marked with triangle and No. 235.

No. 196.—" Two Bacchante Decorating the Bust of Pan." (Height 13″.) Modelled by J. J. Spangler, moulded by Joseph Hill, and marked with his mark △ a triangle. Also Crowned D and Batons with No. 196.

All after the paintings of Angelica Kauffmann. Compare print and picture on plate No. 17.

(All in the Author's Collection.)

PLATE 11

PLATE 12

(Chapter II.)

"Æsculapius." (Height $6\frac{1}{2}''$). Old Derby Biscuit Statuette (No. 99). Modelled by Spängler and used by B. Vulliamy with its companion figure ("Egeria") as ornaments for his Ormolu Clocks and Barometers. Mark No. 99.

(In the Author's Collection.)

PLATE 12

PLATE 13

(Chapter II.)

Beautiful Old Derby Porcelain Biscuit Figure, "The New Diana," No. 120. Modelled by Spängler. (Height $6\frac{1}{2}''$.) This is a very rare figure. It is believed to have been actually moulded and made up by Spangler (in accordance with his agreement with William Duesbury II., to supply "proof" moulding from each model as a copy for the figure makers), as the outer foreleg of the dog is raised, whereas in other examples this is changed to the inner foreleg being raised, so as to minimise the risk of breakage. It also shows signs of inexpert joining up. Mark No. 120.

(In the Author's Collection.)

PLATE 13

PLATE 14

(Chapter II.)

A Charming Old Derby Biscuit Figure, emblematic of "Summer." One of four Derby "Seasons," modelled by Spängler, 7″ high. Marked with Crowned "D" and Batons, the pattern No. 123, a triangle showing it was made by Joseph Hill, and the word "Small" indicating that it was a small size of the set of Seasons which were made in three sizes.

(In the Author's Collection.)

PLATE 14

PLATE 15

(Chapter II.)

Derby Biscuit Figure, with attributes enamelled, of John Wilkes. 12½″ high, *circa* 1780. From model by Stephan.

In Derby Museum.

(By permission of the Corporation.)

PLATE 15

PLATE 16

(Chapter II.)

Beautiful Figure of " A Shepherd," modelled by Coffee, under the personal supervision of Michael Kean, from a classic model.

In the Nottingham Museum.

(By permission of the Corporation.)

PLATE 16

P

PLATE 17

(Chapter II.)

Original Study in Oils by Angelica Kauffmann for her picture of " Cupid Distressed by Three Maidens." And print by W. Wynne Ryland, after Angelica Kauffmann of " Two Bacchante Decorating the Bust of Pan," the originals from which Spängler modelled two of the Old Derby groups shown on plate No. 11.

(In the Author's Collection.)

PLATE 17

PLATE 18

(Illustrating Chapter II.)

Coloured Figure of Old Derby Porcelain of a Gardener, modelled by Spängler. (Height 7½″.)

(In the Author's Collection.)

PLATE 18

PLATE 15

(Illustrating Chapter III. Flower Painters.)

Unique Toilet Ewer and Basin of Crown Derby Porcelain, circa 1790. Painted in colours by William Billingsley with [illegible]. A large group of flowers in centre of Basin. Embossed border in gold and colours. [illegible] Height of Ewer [illegible] inches.

Pattern No. 172 in the Old Derby Pattern Book [illegible] and Book [illegible]. Marked in blue with Crowned [illegible] and Batons; also pattern No. 172.

(In the Author's Collection.)

PLATE 19

(Illustrating Chapter III. Flower Painters.)

Unique Toilet Ewer and Basin of Old Derby Porcelain, *circa* 1793. Painted in colours by William Billingsley, with "A large group of flowers in centre by 'Billensley' with rich border in gold and colours." By Thomas Soar. (Height of Ewer $9\frac{1}{2}''$. Basin $13''$ dia.)

Pattern No. 172 in the Old Derby Pattern Book and Soar's gilder's No. 1. Marked in puce with Crowned *D* and Batons, also pattern No. 172.

(In the Author's Collection.)

PLATE 19

PLATE 20

(Illustrating Chapter III. Flower Painters.)

Enlarged Detail of Group of Flowers on Basin.
Pattern No. 172, painted by Billingsley.

PLATE 20

PLATE 21

(Illustrating Chapter III. Flower Painters.)

Plate exquisitely painted, with a Moss Rose by Quaker Pegg, on Old Derby Porcelain, *circa* 1796. The most beautiful rose ever painted on china. Marked in red, with Crowned *D* and Batons. (Dia. 10″.)

(In the Author's Collection.)

PLATE 21

PLATE 22

(Illustrating Chapter III. Flower Painters.)

Flower Detail Enlargement of William Pegg, the Quaker's Moss Rose.

PLATE 22

PLATE 23

(Illustrating Chapter III. Flower Painters.)

Dessert Plate, 8½″ dia., painted with pink rose, in colours by Edward Withers. Marked in puce with Crowned *D* and Batons. Pattern No. 18 and gilder's No. 2, Joseph Stables.

(In the Author's Collection.)

PLATE 23

PLATE 24

(Illustrating Chapter III. Flower Painters.)

Enlarged detail of Edward Wither's Rose.

PLATE 24

PLATE 25

(Illustrating Chapter III. Flower Painters.)

Plate of a Service of Old Derby Porcelain, *circa* 1820. Painted for "John Trotter, Esq., Durham Park," and marked in gold.

Flowers painted at Derby by Moses Webster.

(Dia. $9\frac{1}{4}''$).

(In the Author's Collection.)

PLATE 25

PLATE 26

(Illustrating Chapter III. Flower Painters.)

Enlarged Flower Detail of Moses Webster's Flower Painting.

PLATE 26

PLATE 27

(Illustrating Chapter IV.)

Dessert Dish of Old Derby Porcelain ($10\frac{1}{2}'' \times 8''$). Painted by Zachariah Boreman, with "View in Dove Dale." It has a broad border of underglaze blue, relieved with very thick rich toned gold scroll-work. Marked with Crowned *D* and batons in blue. Pattern No. 50, and gilder's No., 2. Jos. Stables.

(In the Author's Collection.)

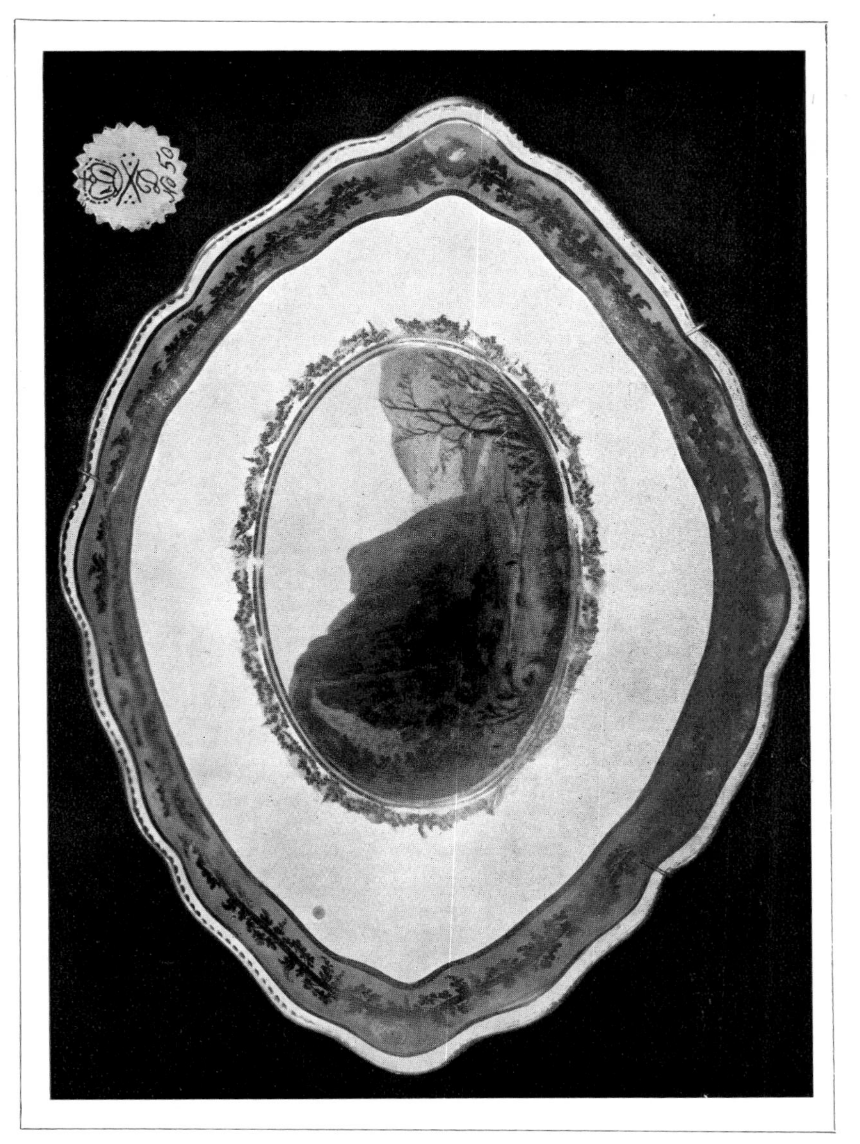

PLATE 27

PLATE 28

(Chapter IV.)

Enlarged Detail of Boreman's Landscape, "View in Dovedale."

PLATE 28

PLATE 29

(Illustrating Landscape Artists.)

Plate of Old Derby Porcelain, painted with a Landscape by Jockey Hill. Marked with Crowned " D " and Crossed Batons in blue, with the pattern No. 67 and the gilder's No. 5.

(In the Derby Museum. By permission of the Corporation.)

PLATE 29

PLATE 30

(Illustrating Landscape Painters.)

Enlarged Detail of Jockey Hill's Landscape.

PLATE 30

PLATE 31

(Illustrating Landscape Painters.)

Old Derby Porcelain Saucer, canary-coloured ground, painted in centre with landscape in colours by Jockey Hill, *circa* 1780.

(In Derby Museum. By permission of the Corporation.)

PLATE 31

PLATE 32

(Illustrating Landscape Painters.)

Enlarged Detail of Landscape Painting on Saucer, by Jockey Hill.

PLATE 32

PLATE 33

(Illustrating Landscape Painters.)

Large Vase of Old Derby Porcelain with Apple Green Ground. Height 11″. Painted with "View in Scotland," by Robert Brewer. Marked in red Crowned *D* with Batons.

(In the Author's Collection.)

PLATE 33

PLATE 34

(Illustrating Landscape Painters.)

Enlarged Detail of Landscape "View in Scotland," by Robert Brewer.

PLATE 34

PLATE 35

(Chapter IV., Illustrating Landscape Painters.)

Plate $9\frac{1}{4}''$ dia. Painted by Zachariah Boreman, in colours, with View of the Bridge and Village of Singleton, near Midhurst, in most Corot-like manner and colouring.

On the back is written in red in script characters :—" Singleton, near Midhurst."

(In the Author's Collection.)

PLATE 35

PLATE 36

(Illustrating Chapter V. Figure Subject Painters.)

Plate of Old Derby Porcelain, finely painted with subject of Children Sheltering from a Thunder Storm. By Richard Askew.

(In the Victoria and Albert Museum. By kind permission of the Director.) Marked in puce.

PLATE 36

PLATE 37

(Illustrating Chapter V. Figure Subject Painters.)

Early Derby Porcelain Dish, *circa* 1770-1775. Painted with a Cupid and Swans in rose-pink camaieu, by Richard Askew. Marked in puce.

(In Derby Museum. By kind permission of the Corporation.)

PLATE 37

PLATE 38

(Illustrating Chapter V.)

Plate of Old Derby Porcelain, $9\frac{1}{4}''$ dia., *circa* 1786-1794. Decorated with bands of pea green, alternating with beautifully executed scroll-work in rich toned honey gilding on a white ground. Beautifully painted by Cuthbert Lawton, with sheep, in a $3\frac{1}{2}''$ dia. Landscape, coloured. Marked in blue with a Jewelled Crown over Crossed Batons and "D" with pattern number 268 underneath. This plate is illustrated in the Old Derby Pattern Book, and is the only early plate in the pattern book marked as painted with animals. It is very rare.

Haslem says in "The Old Derby China Factory":—

"No. 268 is a plate with bands of green, and, between the bands, gilding on the white; 'Animals in Colours, $3\frac{1}{2}$ inches,' in the centre."

(In the Author's Collection.)

PLATE 38

PLATE 39

(Illustrating Chapter V. Figure-Subject Painters.)

Studies of Five Cupids in the Clouds, in rose-pink camaieu, by Richard Askew.
These might be multiplied by a hundred. All different and all charming.

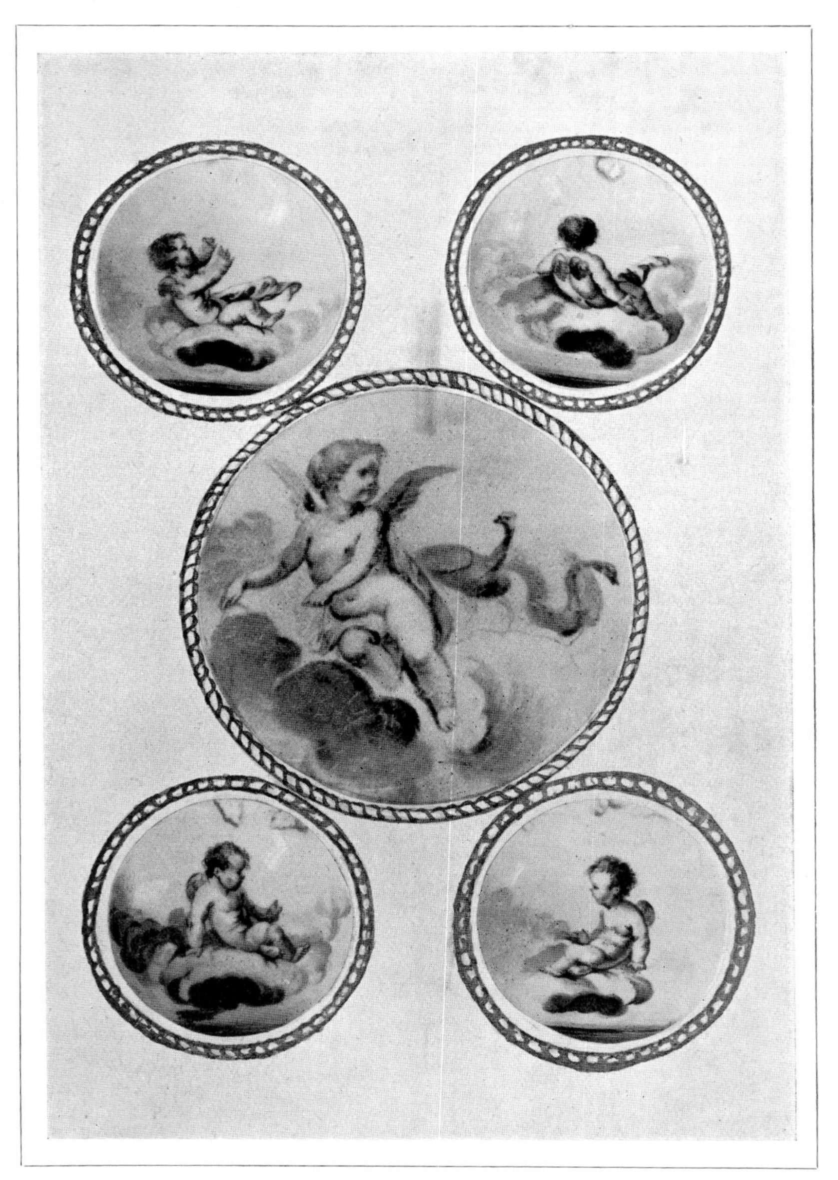

PLATE 39

PLATE 40

(Illustrating Chapter V. Figure-Subject Painters.)

Cabinet Cup of Old Derby Porcelain, painted with Dancing Girl, by James Banford. Marked in puce with Crowned *D* with Batons.

(In Derby Museum. By permission of the Corporation.)

PLATE 40

PLATE 41

(Illustrating Chapter V. Figure-Subject Painters.)

Cabinet Cup and Saucer painted by James Banford, with the "Beggar Girl and Boy" (sometimes "and child"), after Bartolozzi's print of Benwell's picture. No. 216 in the Old Derby Pattern Book. Also the print from which it is copied. Cup marked in puce, saucer in blue. Both in the collection of A. H. S. Bunford, Esq.

PLATE 41

PLATE 42

(Illustrating Chapter V. Figure-Subject Painters.)

Large Vase of Old Derby Porcelain (Height 11″), with dark blue ground. Modelled by Rossi. Richly gilded by Keys. And painted in a reserve with a Cupid with emblems in the Clouds, by John Brewer. Marked in red, with Crowned "D" with Batons, Crown being jewelled.

(In the Author's Collection.)

PLATE 42

PLATE 43

(Illustrating Chapter V. Figure-Subject Painters.)

Enlarged Detail of John Brewer's Painting of a Cupid in the Clouds, on large blue ground vase.

PLATE 43

PLATE 44

(Illustrating Chapter V. Figure-Subject Painters.)

A Pair of Fine Vases (height $11\frac{1}{4}''$), and Covers in Pea Green and Gold, with beautifully modelled flowers by Stephan, and Cupids in Clouds in rose-pink camäieu, painted by Richard Askew, about 11″ high. These are lot 68 in the April 19th, 1771 Catalogue. Duesbury's London Sale.

(In the Author's Collection.)

PLATE 44

PLATE 45

(Illustrating Chapter VI. Bird and Fruit Painters.)

Coffee Cup of Old Derby Porcelain, beautifully painted, with a bird in subdued colouring, by Zacariah Boreman.

(In the Author's Collection.)

PLATE 45

PLATE 46

(Illustrating Chapter VI. Bird and Fruit Painters.)

Old Derby Porcelain Pastille Burner, with perforated cover. Painted with birds by Complin. Mark in puce.

(In Derby Museum. By permission of the Corporation.)

PLATE 46

PLATE 47

Toilet Vase and Stopper of Old Derby Porcelain. Painted with flowers in colours on gold ground, by James Turner. Marked in red. Height $4\frac{1}{8}''$.

(In the Author's Collection.)

PLATE 47

PLATE 48

(Illustrating Chapter VI. Bird and Fruit Painters.)

Plate of Derby Porcelain, with celeste blue ground and fine Arabesque gilding, exquisitely painted with birds in brilliant colours in a softly pencilled river landscape background, by Richard Dodson, *circa* 1810. (Dia. $8\frac{3}{4}''$).

A perfect example of his painting at its best. The gilding is by Torkington. Mark in red. Crowned D with Batons and gilder's No. 7.

(In the Author's Collection.)

PLATE 48

T

PLATE 49

(Illustrating Chapter VI. Bird and Fruit Painters.)

Enlarged Detail of Panel of Birds in Landscape on Dodson's Plate.

PLATE 49

PLATE 50

(Illustrating Chapter VI. Bird and Fruit Painters.)

Mug and Pastille Burner of Old Derby Porcelain, painted with fruit and flowers, by Thomas Steele.

(In Miss Hurlbutt's possession.)

PLATE 50

PLATE 51

Shell-Shaped Comport of Old Derby Porcelain, painted with a "View in Wales," by Daniel Lucas, sen., *circa* 1825. Marked in red. ($9\frac{3}{4}'' \times 9\frac{3}{4}''$.)

(In the Derby Museum. By permission of the Corporation.)

PLATE 51

PLATE 52

(Chapter VII.)

Finely Decorated Cup and Saucer of Old Derby Porcelain, with Rose du Barry ground. Decorated in the Sevres manner. Bloor period. Marked " Bloor Derby " in a circle surrounding a crown, on the saucer, and a Crowned " D " with Batons and the pattern No. 83 on the cup respectively. Both in red.

(In the Author's Collection.)

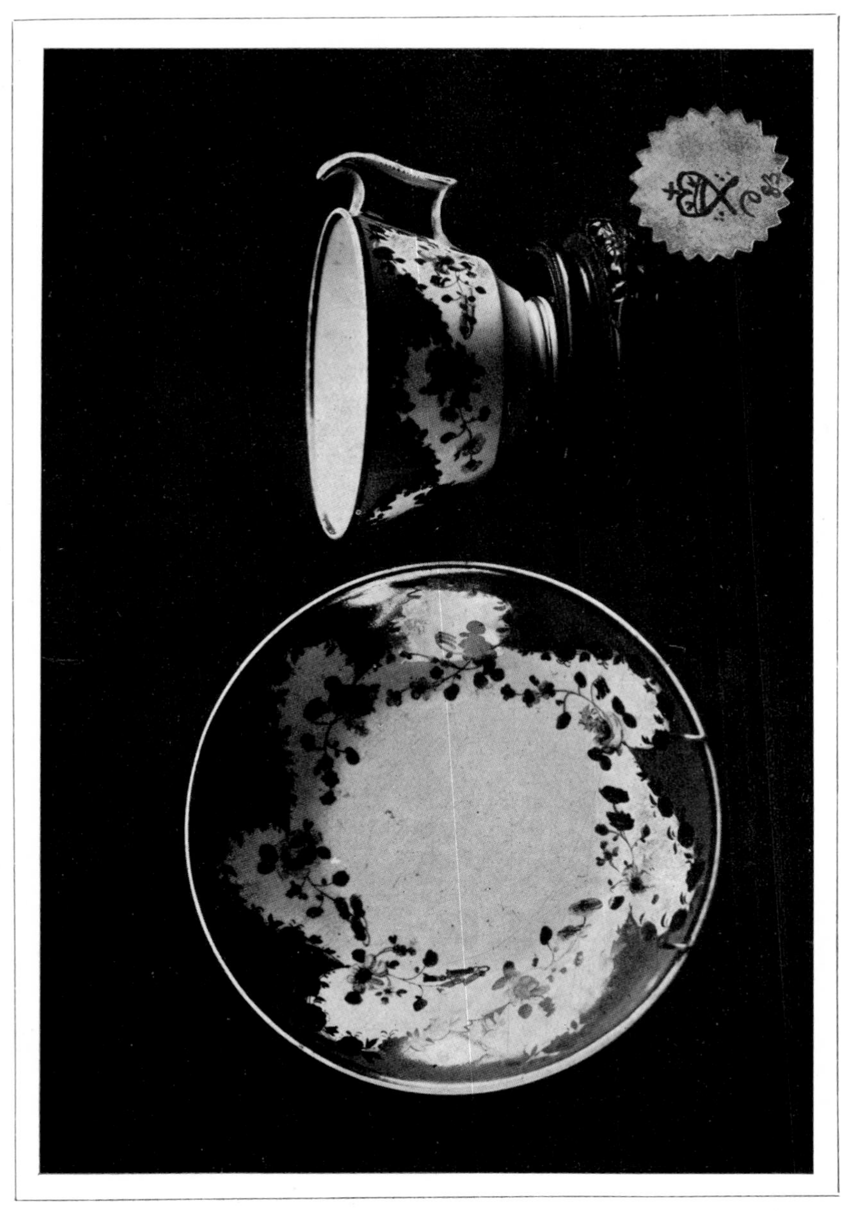

PLATE 52

PLATE 53

(Chapter VII.)

Old Derby Porcelain Pastille Burner, 3½″ high, *circa* 1800-1810. Finely painted with continuous hunting scene, by Cuthbert Lawton. Mark in red.

(In the Derby Museum. By permission of the Corporation.)

PLATE 53

PLATE 54

(Chapter VII.)

Dish of Old Derby Porcelain, painted with a group of flowers, by Billingsley, *circa* 1790-1795. Marked with a Crowned "D" and Batons in puce with pattern No. 127.

(In the Derby Museum. By permission of the Corporation.)

PLATE 54

PLATE 55

(Chapter VII.)

Enlarged Detail of Flowers on Billingsley's Dish, plate No. 54, together with copy of drawing in Billingsley's Sketch Book, from which the flowers in the group are copied, put side by side for purposes of comparison.

(The dish in Derby Museum, the sketch from Bemrose's "Bow, Chelsea, and Derby Porcelain," by kind permission of Messrs Bemrose & Sons, Ltd., Derby.)

PLATE 55

PLATE 56

(Chapter VII.)

Large Vase (11″ high) of Old Derby Porcelain, with dark blue ground, relieved with rich gilding and having reserve painted with landscape by Robert Brewer, entitled " Near Ensterdam."
Mark in red.

(In the Author's Collection.)

PLATE 56

PLATE 57

Comport of Old Derby Porcelain, with " Thistle from Nun's Green," by Quaker Pegg.
$8\frac{1}{2}'' \times 8\frac{1}{2}''$.

(In the Derby Museum. By permission of the Corporation.)

PLATE 57

PLATE 58

Large Plate of Old Derby Porcelain, painted with "Geranium and Carnation," by Quaker Pegg. Marked in red. (Dia. 10″.)

(In the Author's Collection.)

PLATE 58

PLATE 59

Plate of Old Derby Porcelain, *circa* 1786.
Painted with an Imari pattern in brilliant colouring and gold.
This pattern was also painted on Chelsea and on Worcester Porcelain. (Dia. $9\frac{3}{4}''$).
Marked in puce.

(In the Author's Collection.)

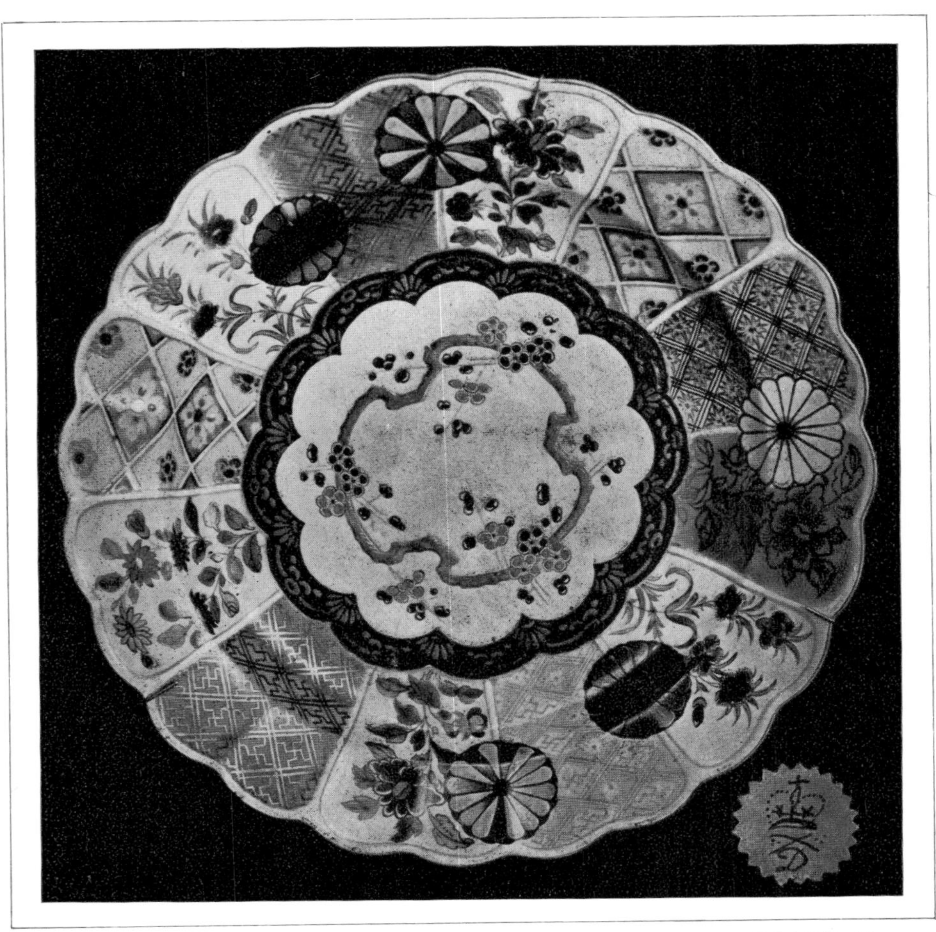

PLATE 59

London, 35, 39, 46, 47, 66, 79, 87, 93, 106, 108, 112, 116.
Longdon, 32.
Longton Hall, 7, 8, 28, 55, 105, 108, 134
Lowestoft, 55, 108.
Lucas, Danl., 14, 113.
Lygo, 33, 35, 40, 44, 45, 68, 69.

M

Madeley, 121.
Mansfield, 70.
Marks, 17-19, 21, 26-28, 52, 59, 64, 72, 75, 80, 89, 92, 96, 100, 110, 111, 116, 121, 124, 132, 133, 135, 138.
Mecklenberg, Duke of, 112.
Meissen, 6, 25, 65, 67, 105, 137.
Meteyard, Eliza, 30.
Mintons, 142.
Models, 15, 29, 31, 32, 36, 40, 41, 48, 51, 52.
Museums, 18, 44, 49.
Morris, 79.

N

Nankin Porcelain, 20, 21.
Nantgarw, 65, 70, 78, 79.
Napoleonic Wars, 13.
Nightingale, 86.
Nottingham Road Factory, 7, 8.

O

Old Hands, 11.
O'Neale, 56, 107, 108.

P

Pallissy, Bernard, 66.
Pardoe, R., 79.
Pattern Numbers (Old Derby Pattern Book), 58, 61, 74, 76, 92, 96, 99, 111, 116, 118, 138, 139.
Pegg, William the younger, 79, 81.
Pegg, William the Quaker, 11, 56-61, 71, 81, 91, 140.
Pitt, William the younger, 31.
Pinxton, 65, 70, 78, 79.
Planché, Andrew, 5, 6, 7, 8.
Plymouth, 108.
Pollard, 79.

Q

Queen Charlotte, 112.

R

Ramsgate, 36.
Rivett, Thos., 5.
Robertson, 113.
Robins & Randall, 79.
Rockingham, 142.
Rodney, Lord, 31.
Rossi, 56, 126.
Roubilliac, 25, 26.

S

Sanby, Paul, 122.
Sèvres, 65, 67, 86, 105, 113.
Sims, 106, 108, 112.
Smith's Blue, 16, 20.

Sheffield, Wm. E., 12, 13.
Snowdon, 87.
Soar, Thos., 12, 32, 56, 71, 131.
Spängler, J. J., 27-29, 32-46, 49, 51, 52, 56.
Sprimont, Nicolas, 29, 85, 86, 112, 129, 136.
St. Cloud, 6.
St. Mary Bridge, 8.
Stables, Wm., 12.
Stanesby, John, 81, 113, 136.
Staffordshire, 30, 65.
Stephan, Pierre, 28-33, 48, 49, 52, 56.
Steele, Thos., 14, 136, 140, 141.
Stoke-on-Trent, 142.
Stoner, Frank, 15.
Strong, Sir R., 85.
Swansea, 65, 78.
Swinton, 142.

T

Tebo, 26.
Thomason, 15.
Torkington, 135, 136.
Trotter, John, 80.
Turner, Jas., 81.
Turner, J. M. W., 122.

V

Vincennes, 86.
Vulliamy, Bn., 33-35.

W

Waterloo, Battle of, 13.
Webster, Moses, 14, 56, 63, 71, 79, 80, 81.

Wedgwood, Josiah, 30, 93, 95, 119.
Whittaker, 28.
Wilkes, John, 31.
Withers, Edward, 56, 62, 64, 65, 71, 73, 81.
Wollams, 87, 106.
Worcester, 7, 20, 26, 55, 65, 79, 105, 107, 108, 121, 129, 134, 137.
Wright, Jos., of Derby, 48.

Z

Zurich, 33.